psychology
moment by moment

a guide to enhancing your clinical practice
with mindfulness and meditation

ELISE E. LABBÉ, PH.D.

New Harbinger Publications, Inc.

Publisher's Note

This publication is designed to provide accurate and authoritative information in regard to the subject matter covered. It is sold with the understanding that the publisher is not engaged in rendering psychological, financial, legal, or other professional services. If expert assistance or counseling is needed, the services of a competent professional should be sought.

FSC
Mixed Sources
Product group from well-managed forests and other controlled sources
Cert no. SW-COC-002283
www.fsc.org
© 1996 Forest Stewardship Council

Library of Congress Cataloging in Publication Data on file

Labbé, Elise E.
  Psychology moment by moment : a guide to enhancing your clinical practice with mindfulness and meditation / Elise E. Labbé.
     p. cm.
  Includes bibliographical references and index.
  ISBN 978-1-57224-895-3 (pbk.) -- ISBN 978-1-57224-896-0 (pdf ebook)
  1. Mindfulness-based cognitive therapy. 2. Meditation--Therapeutic use. I. Title.
  RC489.M55L33 2010
  616.89--dc22
          2010045908

13   12   11

10 9 8 7 6 5 4 3 2 1   First printing

I fell in love with you, my son, the moment I held you in my arms.
You lived life large, giving yourself to the moment, and always told me to go for it.
In your honor I dedicate this work to you, Joel Richard J. Labbé, 1983–2006.

Contents

Acknowledgments

I had great fun writing this book. Thanks first to Melissa Kirk, who invited me on this journey and taught me a lot about writing and publishing along the way. Jess Beebe, I am grateful for your feedback and helping me translate research and practice into this book. Jasmine Star, thank you for the detailed and gritty work you did to help me make this book better than I could have on my own.

I am grateful for my graduate students who kept me on my toes and cheered me on: Jessica Shenesey, Brittany Escuriex, Melissa Womble, Ryan Cochran, and Jay Champagne. Thanks to Sr. Ann Henkel, my spiritual director and "big sister," who not only helps remind me of the important things in life but told me I'd better write this book! Thanks to Dr. Cay Welsh, my dear friend, other "big sister," and fellow mindfulness practitioner, for her faith in me.

Thanks to Dr. Andrée Betancourt, my oldest daughter and grammar queen, who read the manuscript and gave me feedback and encouragement while bringing my first grandchild into the world. Thanks to John Betancourt for his enthusiastic endorsement of my work and a glass of wine to enjoy. Thanks also to my parents, George and Cha Labbé, who taught me about openheartedness. It has been good to have my little sister, Barbara Labbé Gaddy, as a kind sounding board for my ideas and projects. Thanks to my daughter Calley, who reminds me to stop and smell the roses and who is an expert at being in the moment. I appreciate Brittany Roybal's quiet support and willingness to help out when needed. I am grateful for Cosmo, my oldest son; together we have plumbed the depths of sadness and in the process found great joy. I also thank him for his awesome help and expertise in all things technical, including developing my website, www.eliselabbe.com. I am grateful for Ross, my youngest child, as he frequently looked over my shoulder while I was writing this book and surprised me daily with his eagle eye and words of wisdom. I am most grateful for my husband, Bruce Coldsmith, who has encouraged me at every step of the way and challenged me to hang in there through the inevitable crisis of faith one encounters in such a journey.

Foreword

I had the pleasure of meeting Elise Labbé so long ago I am sure neither of us wishes to remember exactly when. Although I cannot remember the date, I vividly recall my first impressions of her, which have endured. Here was a bright, talented scientist-scholar; someone more mature than her young age would suggest; someone who would be going places. At that time, we were engaged in similar research endeavors, and that alone might have accounted for my interest in following her work and budding career. However, there was more than that. I was witnessing her growing in stature, expanding her reach, and accomplishing more than is typical in the academic setting. Our research interests have diverged somewhat over the years, and our paths no longer cross as often as I wish. When she and her publisher asked me to prepare a foreword for this text, my answer was an enthusiastic yes. Here was my chance to catch up with her current work. The timing could have been better. I had just accepted a new position at the University of Memphis and was busy wrapping up my term as president of a national scientific society. For anyone else, I would have had to decline. In fact, I tried to convince myself to pass on this opportunity. But, for Professor Labbé, I simply had no choice. And having read this text, it is clear I made the right choice. I predict with confidence that readers will feel likewise.

Why am I so enthusiastic about her book? Why could I not put it down? Here are just a few of the reasons. In many academic endeavors, scientists do science and practitioners do practice, and never the twain shall meet. Neither group seems to fully appreciate or understand the other. Each camp has well-articulated reasons for staying within the safe confines of their boundaries. Professor Labbé, thankfully, is a member of a new group of professionals, a group that firmly believes these two camps must meet around the campfire—no, not singing "Kumbaya" and pretending differences do not exist, but discussing these differences, learning from one another, translating the findings of science to effective practice, and seeking feedback from those in practice to make sure the translations reflect what the practitioners believe is truly important. Professionals who are likely to be most successful in bridging these camps are people like Professor Labbé, who is deeply familiar with the science as well as the practice. She knows what the science says to do and she knows how to implement the science in real-world settings. Further, she has that unique gift of being able to instruct in a way that is understandable to people at all levels. Mindfulness and related approaches are quite popular, and books abound. Many begin with the premise "This is what I believe" or "This is what I have found works." Professor Labbé takes a refreshing approach, going where the science takes her.

As a child, I remember elders telling me things like "Stop and smell the roses" and "The journey is more important than the destination." All of this sounded nice. How could anyone disagree with that advice? Yet, no one could answer my question about how this was best accomplished. Well, after reading this book, you will have lots of answers, answers grounded in science and tempered with Professor Labbé's wealth of clinical experience. My intent in this foreword is only to whet your appetite. I leave it to Professor Labbé to serve up the dishes. Savor the chapters to come. You certainly will not regret it—and you may just learn things of value not only to the clients you serve but to yourself as well.

—Frank Andrasik, Ph.D.
Distinguished Professor and Chair
Department of Psychology
University of Memphis

Introduction: It Begins with the Breath

Breathe in. Breathe out. Notice your breath without trying to change your breathing. Just be aware of breathing in and breathing out. This is the best place to start your journey into mindfulness.

So quickly we forget that the only thing we *really need* in the moment is to breathe. Realizing and deeply understanding this essential truth opens the door to radical change, happiness, and freedom. I hope to take you on a journey that can help you and your clients find the freedom to breathe, change, and be happy.

Your first breath as you left your mother's womb represents the beginning of your life, opening the door to learning to be fully present in the moment. When you were young, it was easier to be present in the moment. As you grew, you began developing attitudes and beliefs that slowly wrapped you up in false bindings of needs and desires to be separate and independent. With patience and openheartedness, you can learn to loosen these wrappings by practicing mindfulness.

In using mindfulness with my clients, I find that I am most effective when my own mindfulness practice is strong. I encourage you to experiment with the mindfulness techniques for yourself before you present them to your clients.

EVIDENCE-BASED PRACTICE

I am a professor of psychology and a clinical psychologist. I teach and engage in research and clinical practice. One of my passions is trying to figure out how my and others' research results can translate into practice and how my clinical practice can inform science. Using an evidence-based approach in my clinical practice helps me make that flow of information possible. So throughout this book, I weave in research results that can enhance your understanding of how and why mindfulness can help your clients change. I also describe some specific clinical practices that can help improve your skills in obtaining objective evidence regarding the effectiveness of your clinical work. I hope this information can help you improve the effectiveness of mindfulness-based interventions that you use with your clients.

MINDFULNESS-BASED APPROACHES

Many of the new books on mindfulness combine mindfulness with other approaches, such as cognitive behavioral therapy (CBT), acceptance and commitment therapy (ACT), and dialectical behavior therapy (DBT). This can be confusing for professionals who are interested in implementing mindfulness in their practice independent of these approaches or in different contexts. The focus of this book is on "classic" mindfulness and theoretical models that attempt to explain the effectiveness of mindfulness. I draw on Jon Kabat-Zinn's exceptional understanding of mindfulness and his ability to translate concepts related to mindfulness into Western clinics and medical settings (Kabat-Zinn, 1990, 1994, 2005).

The first two chapters of this book provide a brief introduction to the history of mindfulness and to mindfulness concepts. They also provide definitions of mindfulness and problems in attempts to define it. You can better understand the mindfulness techniques in the context of therapy if you understand some of the current models of mindfulness that attempt to explain why and how it works. Therefore, I will briefly present evidence-based support for the mechanisms proposed by these models. To help you illustrate to your clients why and how mindfulness can have positive effects in their everyday lives, I'll describe mindfulness-based strategies in detail and, when available, research support for these strategies.

AN OVERVIEW OF THE BOOK

I hope you begin reading this book at the beginning. As mentioned, the first two chapters will give you the theoretical and contextual information you'll need to explain to your clients why mindfulness-based approaches might be helpful for them. The rest of the chapters build on each other as I take you on a journey that will help you integrate mindfulness into your clinical practice. After you read all of the chapters, you'll be able to more effectively zero in on chapters for different purposes that you might have.

Chapter 3 presents general and practical information on choosing mindfulness techniques and implementing them with your clients. I include guidance on how to practice in the office setting and discuss how you might conduct mindfulness in a group format and provide mindfulness-based retreats for your clients. Chapter 4 explains formal mindfulness techniques. You'll learn how to guide your clients through a variety of formal practices: breathing meditation, the body scan, various sitting meditations, loving-kindness meditation, and walking meditation. Chapter 5 describes informal mindfulness techniques and offers instructions for a wide range of informal practices: mindfulness in daily activities, describing and observing, sensory exercises, awareness of posture, yoga, and using poetry and inspirational writings.

Chapter 6 gives you methods of measuring mindfulness that will be useful in evaluating and documenting important changes in client mindfulness. In the past decade, researchers have developed several measures of mindfulness in response to the need to assess whether individuals really do become mindful after participating in mindfulness-based interventions. Most of these measures assess trait, or dispositional, mindfulness; one measures state mindfulness. (*Trait mindfulness*, or *dispositional mindfulness*, is a person's general tendency to be mindful. A person's *state mindfulness* will fluctuate over time and can vary in intensity in response to the current moment.) In chapter 6 I'll also take a look at concerns in developing mindfulness measures, including issues related to defining mindfulness. Three frequently used mindfulness measures are described, along with their suggested uses and their strengths and weaknesses in measuring mindfulness.

It's exciting that researchers are beginning to study specific mindfulness-based treatment protocols for specific populations and problems. Chapter 7 provides a road map to help you develop mindfulness-based treatment protocols that are evidence-based. Chapters 8 and 9 offer up-to-date information on mindfulness-based protocols for specific populations and problems. Effective, evidence-based mindfulness protocols for children, older adults, and couples are discussed in chapter 8. Chapter 9 describes evidence-based mindfulness protocols for chronic illness, pain, stress; anxiety disorders; depression; and eating disorders.

The final two chapters cover issues related to delivering successful mindfulness-based programs. Chapter 10 offers guidance on developing or furthering your own mindfulness practice. Chapter 11 provides useful methods for systematically assessing evidence-based protocols and guidance on developing effective evaluation procedures. This is important, for if you are to be successful in helping your clients improve, you must be able to evaluate the effectiveness of your interventions. Using the feedback from evaluation, you can then adapt or change your protocols. The information you obtain will also help you grow your mindfulness-based practice. Chapter 11 takes a look at new and exciting programs for adapting mindfulness to several nonclinical venues: the business world, sport and exercise, and education. Many of these new approaches focus on preventing dysfunction or enhancing current functioning rather than curing a problem.

COMING BACK TO THE BREATH

Sometimes I get so excited about using mindfulness to help other people that I forget about my breath and get lost in the doing. Remember to breathe as you read this book. Pause frequently to take a breath and become aware of the present moment. Also remember to breathe and be patient as you introduce mindfulness to your clients. A life of mindfulness is grounded in the moment and deepens each time you breathe, as you sit in quiet. Make it your intention to bring your attention, with loving-kindness, to all of your daily activities and interactions with others, moment by moment.

chapter 1

Mindfulness Concepts

In this chapter I discuss the origins of mindfulness and provide a brief overview of its religious and spiritual roots and its use in contemporary psychological work. I present definitions of mindfulness and related concepts. I also describe current theoretical models of mindfulness and discuss the evidence supporting the mechanisms proposed by these models.

HISTORY OF MINDFULNESS

Mindfulness has become a topic of great interest to clinicians and scientists in recent years. In the past decade there has been an explosion of research on mindfulness, as well as a proliferation of new mindfulness-based interventions. But where did mindfulness come from, and how did it become so interesting to Western clinicians and researchers?

"Mindfulness" is an English translation of the Pali word *sati*, which means "awareness" or "bare attention." (The Buddha's teachings were first written in Pali.) Mindfulness involves the practice of meditation and other techniques and strategies to enhance paying attention on purpose in the present moment. Over 2,500 years ago, the Buddha taught mindfulness. These teachings, which encouraged developing mindfulness and underscored the importance of practice, are now being incorporated into mindfulness-based interventions. To understand mindfulness from within the context of Buddhism, you must understand its relationship to the eightfold path, which the Buddha described as the way to alleviate suffering (Siegel, Germer, & Olendzki, 2009). The eight aspects of the path are right view, intention, speech, action, livelihood, effort, mindfulness, and concentration. Mindfulness isn't as effective if not practiced within this broader context. Ronald Siegel and his colleagues give this example: "It is difficult to sustain mindful awareness if we are causing harm to ourselves or others, or if we do not have the concentration and beneficial intentions to focus our efforts. In other words, it's hard to have a good meditation session after a busy day of cheating, stealing, and killing" (2009, p. 33).

Important differences exist between Eastern and Western psychologies, particularly in regard to their view of the mind. Eastern traditions view the primary focus of introspective inquiry to be the mind and consciousness, which are thought to be the source of human suffering and happiness (Walsh & Shapiro, 2006). Western psychology, on the other hand, views external stimuli as significant causes of human experience. Another important difference is that the Eastern concept of mindfulness emphasizes the unity of mind and body, whereas Western approaches view the mind and body as separate entities. From an Eastern perspective, the experiences of the body's senses are essential for cognitive and emotional understanding. In addition, from an Eastern perspective there is no differentiation of psychological, philosophical, and spiritual concepts. As a result of all of these differences, Westerners have had a difficult time understanding many of the Eastern perspectives on human experience and cultivating mindfulness.

During the 1960s and 1970s, mental health practitioners often pathologized meditation, and meditation teachers were frequently dismissive of Western psychology and psychotherapy (Walsh & Shapiro, 2006). In the mid-1990s, interest in Eastern psychology and philosophy grew as more translations of Buddhist teachings became available. Over the past two decades, increasing dialogue and research have begun to point to mindfulness as a unifying concept across various Western psychotherapies, as well as between Eastern and Western psychologists and philosophers (Didonna, 2009). Principles of mindfulness that span psychotherapies are that the mind can observe itself and can grow in self-understanding and the capacity to accept experience, view oneself in a nonjudging manner, and experience compassion for the suffering of oneself and others (Didonna, 2009).

I was introduced to Zen Buddhism and meditation in the 1970s, during my undergraduate years. I developed a personal meditation practice, and since that time I have explored several different styles of meditation practice for my own growth. As a clinical psychologist, I was trained in cognitive behavioral and evidence-based approaches, and I didn't initially integrate meditation into my clinical practice. However, I did use a variety of self-regulation techniques with my clients, such as biofeedback, autogenic training, hypnosis, self-hypnosis, and progressive relaxation training. It was not until the early 2000s, when I was introduced to Jon Kabat-Zinn's work on mindfulness-based stress reduction (MBSR), that I began to explore integrating mindfulness into my work with clients. I also started teaching my psychology graduate students mindfulness-based interventions from an evidence-based perspective and developed a research program on mindfulness. It seems that my story of embracing mindfulness as an important conceptual, clinical, and research topic parallels the story of many clinicians and researchers over the past two decades.

Mindfulness-based interventions encourage clients to observe their perceptions, sensations, and emotions without identifying with them. In mindfulness meditation, the mind and body actively interact in a way that helps people see themselves as a whole living being in continuous interaction with their internal world (Didonna, 2009). Mindfulness fosters the understanding that the mind and the body are not separate entities, and that states of health and illness don't belong separately to the mind or the body, but to the whole person. The whole person must attend to the present moment. This allows clients to develop a more accurate understanding of their state so they can make better behavioral and cognitive choices in order to improve health and decrease illness.

DEFINING MINDFULNESS

Jon Kabat-Zinn defines mindfulness as "waking up and living in harmony with oneself and the world. It has to do with examining who we are, with questioning our view of the world and our place in it, and with cultivating some appreciation for the fullness of each moment we are alive. Most of all, it has to do with being in touch" (Kabat-Zinn, 1994, p. 3). I use this definition of mindfulness in this book. I'll discuss different aspects of this definition so that you can improve your own understanding of mindfulness and better explain to your clients what mindfulness is and how it can affect their lives. I'll also outline some of the problems in defining mindfulness, address questions related to mindfulness as a spiritual practice, and take a look at mindfulness as a process and an outcome.

Problems in Defining Mindfulness

Mindfulness presents a challenge to scientists who try to define it. From an evidence-based perspective, scientists have to attempt to define concepts in a specific and objective manner. Researchers call this an *operational definition*. Psychology has quite a history of studying concepts that are difficult to define operationally—for example, depression, self-esteem, anger, and personality. However, if practitioners and researchers are to gain insight and study evidence for these concepts that resist definition, they must start somewhere, with the realization and acceptance that they will never be able to define these concepts completely. An evidence-based approach to defining mindfulness provides an alternative to defining concepts objectively. An evidence-based approach to the study of mindfulness has been successful in developing mindfulness-based interventions for treating or preventing a variety of health problems. Practitioners can have confidence in using these evidence-based interventions with their clients. And even though professionals often appreciate the idea that mindfulness attempts to do away with false distinctions, they have to realize that for mindfulness to gain acceptance as an evidence-based intervention, an empirical approach is necessary. This means that professionals must attempt to define mindfulness in ways that are measurable. Several definitions of mindfulness have been used in the research literature, and it is important to keep in mind that any definition discussed will be inadequate in some regards and probably controversial (Bishop et al., 2004).

Mindfulness and Spirituality

Jon Kabat-Zinn (1994) points out that while mindfulness is an ancient Buddhist practice, it is relevant to us today regardless of whether or not we practice Buddhism. Most Western mental health professionals focus on describing and teaching mindfulness skills to their clients without including any discussion of mindfulness from a religious or spiritual perspective (Baer, 2006). In my studies of spirituality, I find that most religions offer various aspects of mindfulness in their teachings (Labbé, 2009; Labbé & Fobes, 2010). If you have a spiritual practice based on any of the major world religions, you might find yourself relating easily to some aspects of mindfulness, especially when I review mindfulness qualities and, later in the book, mindfulness techniques.

When I teach mindfulness, my graduate students often remark that it feels spiritual to them. In clinical settings, clients may report that participating in mindfulness exercises was a spiritual experience. My response to students and clients is to be open to and validate their reports. But for the purposes of this book, and from an evidence-based perspective, I will consider mindfulness to be a secular practice and an approach to self-regulation. Kabat-Zinn (1994) reports that he tries to avoid using the term "spiritual" when discussing mindfulness, as there are so many different meanings associated with the term that can confuse a person's understanding or expectations of mindfulness. Furthermore, in most health care practices it may be inappropriate to discuss "spiritual" aspects of an individual's functioning.

Another concern with referring to mindfulness as spiritual relates to the idea that mindfulness is based on an integrated view of human experience, whereas categorization of mind, body, and spirit tends to suggest that these aspects of our experience are independent. Referring to mindfulness as spiritual implies that it is distinct or separate from the functioning of the body and mind. From a mindfulness-based perspective, the practitioner wants to help clients understand that buying into this concept of mind, body, and spirit as distinct entities can lead to health problems. For example, if a client is busy planning and thinking about all he needs to do and as a result doesn't pay attention to physical symptoms of stress, he might not notice that he's getting sick and needs to care for his body. He may not make the connection that his mental state—worry—is affecting the functioning of his physical state, as the two are intimately connected. Health psychology research consistently supports the idea that psychological problems are risk factors for chronic illness (Taylor, 2008). An example is research demonstrating that anxiety can trigger headaches and that learning to cope with anxiety can reduce the frequency of headaches (Labbé, 1999).

Mindfulness as a Process and an Outcome

Mindfulness is a simple, commonsense approach to life. The challenge is to be consistently mindful. In fact, even mindlessness can be an opportunity to become more mindful. Mindfulness requires a lifestyle change that involves a person's cognitive, behavioral, physiological, and emotional response to every moment. A mindfulness approach to understanding human experience considers each person as a whole being and emphasizes that any attempt to separate or compartmentalize aspects of ourselves only leads to a false understanding of human nature. Furthermore, each being is not separate from any aspect of life and the universe; again, seeing an individual as a truly separate being leads to a false understanding of life.

Mindfulness involves paying attention in a certain way (Kabat-Zinn, 1990). Those who practice mindfulness direct their attention to the present moment in a nonjudging and accepting manner. Several other qualities of mindfulness can influence this attending to the present moment that distinguishes mindfulness from other ways of paying attention. I'll discuss these mindfulness qualities in the next section.

Kabat-Zinn proposed that mindfulness is the "common pathway of what makes us human, our capacity for awareness, and for self-knowing" (2005, p. 11). He maintains that paying attention and engaging in mindfulness meditation enhances mindfulness. In 2003, Kirk Brown and Richard Ryan defined mindfulness as being aware of whatever is present in each moment, noting that the person could be aware of a thought, sensation, worry, or anything else that may be taking place.

Shauna Shapiro and Linda Carlson suggested that mindfulness can be defined as a process as well as an outcome. Mindfulness can refer to mindful awareness or to the practice of being mindful. They make the distinction between "big *M* mindfulness" and "little *m* mindfulness" (2009, pp. 4-8). Big *M* refers to mindful awareness: a deep awareness of one's whole self in each moment. Furthermore, mindful awareness is an open attention to what is, without preconceived notions. This open attention creates a freedom in one's understanding of self, others, and the universe. Little *m* refers to the mindfulness practice. Little *m* involves a purposeful approach to experience with the intention of fostering big *M*.

Scientists will continue to explore and define mindfulness. At this time, most would probably agree that mindfulness is paying attention in a particular way to all that one experiences moment to moment. Certain cognitive and emotional qualities influence the particular way one attends to present experience.

MINDFULNESS QUALITIES

Mindfulness qualities are cognitive and affective responses that are cultivated as we attend to the present moment. Engaging these qualities creates a powerful intrapersonal and interpersonal effect. These qualities overlap with and enhance other qualities within ourselves as well as our interactions with other people and the universe. Mindfulness qualities can be directly presented to the client as important concepts to explore and meditate on. You can use personal examples and stories from others, including individuals who are masters of mindfulness, to help facilitate your clients' understanding of these qualities. Sometimes poems, metaphors, or inspirational quotes are used to help clients understand these qualities. Specific mindfulness meditations and strategies build and strengthen mindfulness qualities. Some strategies or techniques focus on a particular mindfulness quality, while others can foster all of the qualities.

Cognitive Qualities of Mindfulness

The cognitive qualities of mindfulness most frequently discussed and researched are acceptance, nonjudging, nonstriving, patience, trust, openness, and letting go (Kabat-Zinn, 2005; Shapiro & Carlson, 2009; Nhat Hanh, 1993). Here are brief descriptions of these cognitive qualities (adapted from Shapiro & Schwartz, 2000):

○ **Nonstriving:** not goal oriented; remaining unattached to outcome or achievement

○ **Nonjudging:** impartial witnessing; observing without evaluation and categorization

○ **Acceptance:** being open to seeing and acknowledging things as they are

○ **Patience:** allowing things to unfold in their time in regard to ourselves and others

○ **Trust:** trusting both oneself and the process of the mindfulness practice

○ **Openness:** seeing things as though for the first time; creating possibilities by paying attention to all feedback

○ **Letting go:** nonattachment; not holding on to thoughts, feelings, or experiences

Nonstriving refers to remaining unattached to a particular outcome as one experiences the present moment. It can also refer to not being goal oriented. Thich Nhat Hanh (2000) gives the example of having the goal to get to a particular place when one is driving and how most people, intent on the road ahead and getting someplace on time, will miss the joy of the drive and the moment of now. He emphasizes that being in the present doesn't mean being unconcerned for the past and the future. Because the present is made of the past, the past is alive in the present moment. And because present awareness and choices affect the future, the future also exists in the present. If you take good care of the present moment, you won't have to worry about the future, since the future is being made in the present. Hope can get in the way of being in the present moment because we use up energy thinking about the future instead of being fully energized in the present moment.

Nonjudging involves observing yourself and the world without evaluating, categorizing, or stereo-typing your experiences. As a way to engender discussion, people often ask how you're doing or how your day went, usually expecting a categorical response—good or bad. From a mindful, nonjudging perspective, you would take a breath and reply that it was neither good nor bad; it just was. People often ask limiting questions and expect answers that provide a quick snapshot of the other person's experiences. Unfortunately, we can begin to buy into these judgments and lose important information about our nature and the constantly changing experiences of life. Nonjudging allows us to escape this limited way of viewing the world and opens us up to whatever is happening in the moment.

Acceptance means clearly seeing and embracing things as they are. Most of us can remember vacations or special events that we had anticipated for long periods with high expectations but then resulted in disappointment. On the other hand, you may have had the reverse experience of dreading an event and then having it turn out better than expected. An accepting stance allows us to be free to experience what really is at any given moment and releases us from wasted worry or expectation. Acceptance frees us up to respond to the present moment with honesty and clarity, creating a healthier response to life. Nonjudging and acceptance influence each other, but they are different cognitive processes. Judging creates a sense of separateness from direct experience. Nonjudging, as a cognitive process, attempts to view others and our experiences as unique, without attempting to categorize and judge them as good or bad. Acceptance, on the other hand, allows you to assimilate your experiences into your awareness. Acceptance allows you to reap the benefit of nonjudging and open yourself up to all things, whether they are uncomfortable or enjoyable. Acceptance means you don't give up when experiencing things you dislike or find undesirable. Rather, it allows you to recognize truthfully all aspects of yourself and the world in order to make changes that are more healthful for yourself and others.

Patience refers to acknowledging and accepting the time frame of the natural development of nature, others, ourselves, and situations. A culture of instant gratification in everything from entertainment to information to food weakens our ability to wait patiently. We become impatient with others and ourselves, creating unnecessary frustration, anger, and anxiety. Kabat-Zinn (1990) gives the example of a child who tries to help a butterfly out of its chrysalis by breaking it open. Unfortunately, the butterfly is harmed in the process. Kabat-Zinn encourages clients to be intentionally patient with their symptoms. When they are frustrated because of lack of progress in reducing symptoms, he reminds them to give themselves room for their current experiences. When the mind becomes agitated, patience allows us the freedom to be still and to quiet the mind. Patience allows things to unfold in their own time, just as letting the butterfly emerge on its own is the only way for it to become a butterfly.

Trust involves trusting ourselves to learn and grow by paying attention in the present moment. We must also place our trust in the process of mindfulness practice. Kabat-Zinn describes trust as "a feeling of confidence or conviction that things can unfold within a dependable framework that embodies order and integrity" (1994, p. 58). Trust in the now fosters self-trust and the ability to develop our capacity for mindfulness. By paying attention and spending time in silence listening to ourselves, we are likely to discover that we know more about the world and ourselves than we think we do. When we trust in our basic wisdom, we might make mistakes, but by paying attention with kindness to these mistakes, we can learn and make better choices in the future. You are your own person, and ultimately you have to trust yourself, even in cultivating your own mindfulness. As you grow in self-trust, your trust in others will also grow.

Openness means developing a quality sometimes referred to as beginner's mind. Openness creates the possibility of paying attention to all stimuli, both within and outside ourselves. This means letting go of preconceived ideas, beliefs, and attitudes about experiences. An open stance allows us to "wake up" to the present moment and experience a new awareness of ourselves and the world. Thich Nhat Hanh (2000) gives the example of "flower fresh" meditation, in which you open yourself to seeing others as they are in the present moment.

Letting go is a conscious decision to release thoughts, feelings, or experiences. Letting go is also referred to as nonattachment to self and the world. Nonattachment should not be confused with not enjoying present-moment experiences, as it does not mean being detached from that experience. Nonattachment differs from detachment in that you recognize your feelings and thoughts, whereas in detachment you separate feelings from thoughts and repress them. Letting go means understanding the temporary nature of all things and not clinging to feelings, thoughts, things, and other beings. Letting go or nonattachment doesn't mean you can't have goals, values, and possessions or move along a certain path in your life. What it does mean is not holding on to those values, goals, possessions, or paths so tightly that you sacrifice paying attention in the moment and the opportunity to be in touch with what is. Letting go provides greater awareness so that you can make healthier choices for yourself and the world.

Affective Qualities of Mindfulness

The five affective qualities of mindfulness most often discussed and studied are generosity, empathy, gratitude, gentleness, and loving-kindness (Kabat-Zinn, 2005; Shapiro & Schwartz, 2000; Nhat Hanh, 2000). These feelings may result when we attend to the present moment with the cognitive qualities described above. In turn, fostering these emotional responses will enhance your ability to see and attend more clearly in the present moment. Here are brief descriptions of these affective qualities (adapted from Shapiro & Schwartz, 2000):

- ○ **Gratitude:** the quality of reverence; appreciating and being thankful for the present moment

- ○ **Gentleness:** characterized by a soft, considerate, and tender quality; soothing but not passive, undisciplined, or indulgent

- ○ **Generosity:** giving within a context of love and compassion, without attachment to gain or thought of return (what's given need not be material)

- ○ **Empathy:** the quality of feeling and understanding another person's situation—their perspectives, emotions, actions, and reactions—and communicating this to the person

- ○ **Loving-kindness:** a quality embodying benevolence, compassion, and cherishing; a quality filled with forgiveness and unconditional love

Gratitude involves being thankful for what exists in the present moment. Gratitude requires you to stop and, in the moment, revere all aspects of life. It embraces the good as well as the bad, and it can grow regardless of current good fortune or adversity. As Kabat-Zinn (2006) says in one of his meditation recordings, "If you are breathing, there is more right with you than wrong." Gratitude can be expressed through action, as well as in giving simple thanks for the precious gift of life.

Gentleness is reflected in responses that are soft, quiet, and light. Gentleness does not imply passivity, giving in to behaviors that aren't healthy, or compromising your values. You can call on gentleness when judgments emerge in your mind about actions, thoughts, and feelings that you might be experiencing. Gentleness helps develop generosity and gratitude and weakens anger, frustration, and guilt.

Generosity is giving to yourself or others with love and concern, and with no expectation for anything in return. You can be generous with service, with things, or with your heart, as well as with your mind. Generosity fosters openness as it allows you to give space to whatever is happening in the present moment.

Empathy is the quality of being able to feel how another person feels without imposing your views or providing judgments on the other person's feelings. Empathy involves communicating to others in such a way that they experience greater understanding of themselves. A good deal of psychological research and theory suggests that empathy is one of the variables in the therapeutic relationship that contributes most to treatment success (Sue & Sue, 2008). Empathy fosters interconnectedness with all beings and helps break down the illusion of separateness that many people experience. Empathy acknowledges that intimate knowledge of others is possible and sets the stage for the healing effects of social support.

Loving-kindness is a complex and joyful response to oneself, others, and the universe. It involves compassion, unconditional acceptance and love, and savoring ourselves and others. Loving-kindness pulls together the other affective qualities in a loving response. It can generate more love, compassion, and forgiveness. Many people report that practicing loving-kindness meditation touches a deep chord within, and that they find themselves experiencing both joy and sorrow, along with a deep, heartfelt appreciation for all beings (Kabat-Zinn, 1990).

Summing Up Cognitive and Affective Qualities of Mindfulness

The mindfulness and affective qualities described above can be encouraged, and interventions can be developed to enhance these qualities. Additional research is needed to assess the long-term "potency" of these qualities in helping people change. Few studies have assessed the level and change in these qualities from pre- to post-intervention. Furthermore, there may be other qualities of mindfulness that have not been fully described or studied.

MODELS OF MINDFULNESS

In this section, I'll present three theoretical models of mindfulness: the intention systemic model (Shapiro & Schwartz, 2000), the attention and awareness model (K. W. Brown, Ryan, & Creswell, 2007a, 2007b), and the developing neuroscientific models. I will describe each model and present examples of relevant research. This is not a comprehensive review of each model; rather, it's a brief summary and review of the evidence base for each model.

Intentional Systemic Mindfulness Model

In 1948, Norbert Weiner introduced cybernetics and applied it to living systems as a model for self-regulation. (*Self-regulation* is how a system regulates itself to achieve specific goals.) Weiner's model presented the idea of nonconscious self-regulation. An example is how the autonomic nervous system adjusts a person's response to stress by initially increasing sympathetic nervous system functioning—increasing heart rate, respiration, and blood flow to large muscles, and so on—then later the parasympathetic system kicks in to bring the body back to homeostasis by decreasing heart rate, respiration, and blood flow to large muscles. Your body responds without having to think about it at a conscious level. You don't have to tell your heart to beat faster or slow down, for example.

In the 1980s, Gary Schwartz argued that self-regulation can also be a conscious process (Schwartz, 1984, 1990). An example of conscious self-regulation is noticing that you're feeling stressed and deciding that it would be helpful to take twenty minutes to meditate.

Shauna Shapiro and Gary Schwartz's intentional systemic mindfulness model (2000) extends Weiner's and Schwartz's models of self-regulation by incorporating mindfulness concepts. *Intentional systemic mindfulness* (ISM) describes mindfulness as conscious, attentional self-regulation. Mindfulness leads to awareness of self-regulation by fostering attention that is consistent with the mindfulness qualities described above: acceptance, nonjudging, nonstriving, patience, trust, openness, and letting go.

Shapiro and Schwartz (2000) suggest that intention is the core of ISM. First, there is the intention to pay attention while employing the mindfulness qualities. This aspect of intention reflects how we should direct our attention. If clients attend to the present moment with a sense of limitation, anxiety, or fear that they aren't doing mindfulness "right," their experience will be characterized by those qualities. But if they attend to the present moment with an attitude of openness, nonjudgment, or gratitude for whatever is happening, their experience will be quite different. Second, we must also pay attention within a systems perspective. An example would be when a client attends to his experience with mindfulness and recognizes himself as being connected to family, friends, and community. He understands that his healing plays a part in healing relationships and develops a greater awareness of how all beings are interconnected and interdependent. A systems perspective on intention reflects why we attend to our present-moment experience, suggesting an awareness of being an integrated whole, as well as being part of a larger integrated system.

Mindfulness practice involves consistent moment-to-moment attention focused on awareness of mental, physical, and emotional responses as these responses enter into awareness. ISM includes intention as an initiating antecedent to attention. The intention to attend consistently while using the mindfulness qualities will improve connections between multiple biopsychosocial pathways within the person. This will result in better regulation of all systems within the body, promoting order within the person and better health. Techniques or skills informed by mindfulness awareness used in self-regulation may more effectively heal a person at the symptom level, as well as all of the other system levels.

ISM provides a way to formulate self-regulation goals from within, which the person can then extend to external systems. ISM also applies the practice of mindful attention to all aspects of the person's experience in order to improve self-regulation. ISM integrates a systemic perspective with mindfulness awareness and practice by delineating both the process and the open attention of mindfulness.

Shapiro and Schwartz (2000) propose that the way we attend to present-moment experience is healing, not just the attention in and of itself. We must attend with the intention to foster the mindfulness qualities as we engage in a self-regulation technique. Attention to biopsychosocial responses without utilizing the mindfulness qualities could result in further ill health or no change at all.

Shapiro and Schwartz (2000) give this example: "If people who attend to their blood pressure attend with fear that they will not be able to control it or with anger at themselves for having high blood pressure, this may have deleterious effects on their health or at least impede the potential healing effects of the self-regulation technique" (p. 262). However, if people with high blood pressure try a new self-regulation technique with the intention to learn it with openness and patience, they may be able to more effectively pay attention and successfully learn the new technique to reduce their high blood pressure.

A more mindful approach to self-care may also foster greater feelings of connectedness with others, due to an increased ability to recognize the interconnectedness of all things. Increased social support and feelings of connectedness may be important aspects of the healing process. Health psychology research consistently finds that social support is one of the best predictors of better health, lower mortality rates, and better response to prevention and treatment for illness (Labbé & Fobes, 2010; Taylor, 2008). Research also indicates that people who perceive they have social support, regardless of whether they actually receive social support, have better health and response to treatment, as well as lower mortality rates. The ISM model predicts that mindfulness in itself promotes connections to others by allowing one to experience the interconnectedness of all things. Mindfulness practice facilitates feelings of connectedness to others that might be lacking in other types of self-regulation interventions.

More broadly, the ISM model provides the systemic perspective that may be missing in other models of self-regulation. From an ISM perspective, it is important to consider healing from multiple levels of systems. Levels range from basic energy systems within the body to family systems to health care systems, and indeed, the entire universe. Each level is integral to the healing process as well as to the whole system; and in turn, changes at each level will influence all other levels.

In conclusion, Shapiro and Schwartz's ISM model is dynamic and allows you to evaluate the influence of a variety of characteristic ways of behaving, feeling, and thinking as clients attend to the present moment. You can use this biopsychosocial model to explain to clients the effects of intending to pay attention with mindfulness, particularly with clients who have chronic illness and pain. ISM helps researchers and practitioners evaluate behavior, feelings, and thoughts that may influence the ability to attend with mindfulness by providing concepts that can be measured and targeted for change. ISM can aid in understanding and developing mindfulness-based methods to improve self-regulation. A key point that differentiates ISM from other models is its emphasis on the systemic nature of mindfulness, allowing for the assessment of the impact of multiple systems on individual functioning, including family and health care systems.

Mindful Attention and Awareness Model

In 2003, Kirk Brown and Richard Ryan defined mindfulness as "receptive attention to and awareness of present events and experience" (p. 212). In their ongoing research, they regard mindfulness as a unique construct and discuss research on mindfulness states and traits and the relationship of mindfulness to other constructs that may overlap with it. Characteristics of mindfulness that they are most concerned with are clarity of awareness; nonconceptual, nondiscriminatory awareness; flexibility of awareness and attention; an empirical stance toward reality; present-oriented consciousness; and stability or continuity of attention (K. W. Brown et al., 2007a). These characteristics overlap with each other and should not be considered as distinct aspects of mindfulness. Brown and his colleagues propose that experimental studies of these characteristics will foster an empirical understanding of mindfulness.

Clarity of awareness is an open and unbiased stance in regard to moment-to-moment experience in all aspects of life. Through bare attention, we can perceive clearly and deeply into ourselves. Clarity of awareness involves recognizing experiences or realities that are painful. When acceptance and nonjudgment are applied to this awareness, we can observe while being less reactive or defensive when experiencing uncomfortable stimuli. Many mindfulness techniques foster clarity of awareness.

Mindfulness involves nonconceptual, nondiscriminatory awareness. This means that a mindful stance doesn't involve immediate evaluation, categorization, or comparison of our moment-to-moment experience. This doesn't mean that mindfulness does not involve thought; rather, it means mindfulness encourages a different relationship with thought. Thoughts are viewed as simply objects of attention, like all other objects of attention. We begin to understand thoughts as thoughts and emotions as reactions to thoughts. This provides more freedom to attend to or disconnect from a thought.

Mindfulness is characterized by flexibility of awareness and attention. You can be aware of all that is in the moment while also being focused on something in particular. Mindfulness promotes fluid movement to and from a larger perspective to focused attention.

A state of mindfulness encourages an empirical stance toward reality. This stance is not disinterested or intellectual but that of a participant observer. Mindfulness allows for the full experience of sensations, thoughts, and feelings without reflective judging or impulsive responses to our experience. Research suggests this empirical stance increases feelings of wholeness and connection to ourselves and others.

Mindfulness is also associated with a present-oriented consciousness. This doesn't mean thoughts of past and future are disregarded or unimportant; rather, the focus is on being fully aware of whatever is present in the moment. Being able to consider experiences and potential future paths for reaching goals is an important function of self-regulation. However, if we aren't able to be in the present moment, we can lose precious knowledge of what is real. Kabat-Zinn (2005) provides many examples of "waking up" to the present moment as one practices mindfulness.

Although mindfulness is an inherent capacity of human beings, it can vary within each individual and between individuals, as can stability and continuity of attention and awareness. Mindfulness is present focused and includes the ability to recognize when we have mentally strayed away from the present. Noticing when we are no longer attending to the present moment is an example of how mindfulness can encompass mindlessness.

Kirk Brown and colleagues (2007a) note that there is a growing body of research suggesting that alerting attention, orienting attention, and executive attention are related to mindfulness. *Alerting attention* is the consistent attention to experience, *orienting attention* is being able to notice important information in one's environment, and *executive attention* is the ability to examine responses and reactions to one's environment (Raz & Buhle, 2006). Research in cognitive neuroscience has shown there is a functional neural network in the brain that guides alerting attention (Robertson & Garavan, 2004). The right dorsolateral prefrontal cortex and the right parietal cortex regulate sustained attention by monitoring and maintaining attention (Robertson & Garavan, 2004). Mindfulness relates conceptually to alerting and orienting attention. Based on new studies in cognitive neuroscience, Brown and colleagues (2007a) propose that mindfulness training can enhance both alerting and orienting attention. For example, some of the studies they cite demonstrate greater cortical thickness in areas of the right prefrontal cortex and right anterior insula among practitioners of mindfulness meditation (Jha, Krompinger, & Baime, 2007; Lazar et al., 2005). The research results suggest that experienced meditators demonstrate sustained attention and awareness and enhanced orientating attention compared to those who don't meditate.

Mindfulness can play a role in enhancing executive attention (K. W. Brown et al., 2007a), which is important for self-regulation. Executive attention functions include monitoring, assessing, and determining behavioral responses to often competing environmental stimuli. Habitual responses can be inhibited through effective executive attention, providing an important pathway for changing maladaptive behavior. Research on executive attention supports the proposal by Kirk Brown and colleagues (2007a) that mindfulness offers an empirical stance on reality. Recent research demonstrates that mindfulness enhances executive attention in both healthy and clinical populations through better behavioral regulation and self-control. An example of such research found that mindfulness engaged executive attentional neural networks (Creswell, Way, Eisenberger, & Lieberman, 2007). This study showed greater prefrontal cortical inhibition of amygdala responses during affect labeling among participants with higher levels of trait mindfulness.

Kirk Brown and colleagues (2007a) provide an empirical approach to understanding and studying mindfulness. While their model is not based on clinical conceptions of mindfulness, it does provide a testable framework for evidence-based evaluation of mindfulness interventions.

Neuroscientific Models

Neuroscientific research on mindfulness focuses on understanding the neural systems that are employed in states of meditation (Treadway & Lazar, 2009). Neuroscientists are also interested in the short- and long-term effects of mindfulness practice on the structure and function of the brain. In recent years, an increasing number of studies have examined the neurobiological and cognitive effects of mindfulness on nonclinical and clinical populations. Neuroscientists are beginning to develop models of the mind-body effects of mindfulness. Early neuroscience research focused on studying individuals who were experts or masters of mindfulness. These studies often involved Buddhist monks and other individuals who had devoted their lives to the practice of mindfulness, people who spent hours each day meditating and intentionally practicing mindfulness-enhancing behaviors. For example, neuroscientists studied Buddhist monks during meditation and found long-distance phase synchrony and gamma wave activity with a higher than normal amplitude (Lutz, Greischar, Rawlings, Ricard, & Davidson, 2004). Long-distance phase synchrony may reflect large-scale neural coordination (Ludwig & Kabat-Zinn, 2008). This is just one example of research that suggests meditation can have beneficial effects on the functioning of the brain.

As neuroscience technologies advance and become less costly, we will probably see more research on mindfulness from a neurocognitive perspective. An example of this type of study was a randomized controlled evaluation of the neurological and immune system effects of a mindfulness meditation training program on healthy employees in a work setting (Davidson et al., 2003). Results of the study indicated significant increases in left-side anterior activation of the brain, along with significant increases in levels of antibodies to influenza vaccines, in meditators compared to nonmeditators. Left-side anterior activation is associated with positive affect. The researchers also found that increased magnitude of left-side activation was predictive of changes in levels of antibodies. This study is noteworthy, as participants were people in a real-world setting and the researchers used two measures of physiological functioning to measure the effects of meditation.

Attention and awareness have become foci of neuroscience research because meditators claim to have increased abilities in both of these mental processes. As referenced in the previous section, Kirk Brown and colleagues (2007a) found that several recent studies support these claims. Another area of interest is examining "beginner's mind" by studying the effects of meditation on habituation (Treadway & Lazar, 2009). A few studies support the idea that meditation practice decreases habituation and increases attentional capacity. Although more research is needed to confirm that mindfulness meditation has a salutary effect on health, a growing number of studies provide positive support for the effects of meditation on attention and habituation.

There is quite a bit of research looking into whether meditative states represent a distinctive state of consciousness. To date, findings have been inconclusive. In 2009, Michael Treadway and Sara Lazar suggested differences in findings may be related to the type of meditation evaluated and differences in study design. Neuroimaging studies may help explain the nature of meditative states, particularly research that examines changes in the structure of the brain. However, drawing conclusions from these studies may present some of the same problems as with earlier studies, because different researchers used different methodologies and meditation practices. But even with these differences, several similar results have been reported across studies. One consistent finding is that the dorsolateral prefrontal cortex is activated across different meditation styles for about 30 percent of the studies reported (Treadway & Lazar, 2009). Treadway and Lazar suggest that meditation causes state changes of increased dorsolateral prefrontal cortex activation, which is associated with increased attention and executive-decision making. In another example of a study examining changes in brain structure, Lazar and colleagues (2005) compared long-term meditators to a control group of participants who didn't meditate. They studied cortical thickness using high-resolution MRI images and found that long-term meditators demonstrated greater cortical thickness in the anterior insula, sensory cortex, and prefrontal cortex compared to the control group.

These results suggest that meditation causes changes in brain structure associated with increased attention and executive-decision making.

Researchers are reporting similar findings on the effects of meditation on neurocognitive systems within the brain that are focused on emotion regulation. They are particularly interested in differentiating positive from negative emotional responses during meditative and nonmeditative states. Studies by Davidson and colleagues (2003) and Creswell and colleagues (2007) provide tentative support that mindfulness is associated with changes in brain functioning that reflect positive affect.

In conclusion, neuroscientific research suggests that meditation is a unique mental state and that it may be associated with long-term functional and structural changes in some regions of the brain. Some of the limitations of the majority of research to date include small numbers of participants, differences in meditative styles, and differences in the type of technology and methodology used to study brain function and structure. Regions of the brain that have been studied are those known to be associated with attention, awareness, and positive affect, all of which are important for health and wellness.

Mindfulness Models and Clinical Practice

I refer to the intentional systemic mindfulness model, the mindful attention and awareness model, and the neuroscientific model throughout the book as they provide a theoretical basis for evaluating mindfulness and developing mindfulness-based interventions. These models are works in progress, and professionals interested in developing an expertise in mindfulness should continue to follow research that supports or points to new models of mindfulness.

These mindfulness models should help you understand some of the theoretical issues related to mindfulness so that you can anticipate potential changes your clients may experience during participation in mindfulness-based interventions. Over the past several years these models have stimulated a good deal of research that supports the beneficial effects of mindfulness-based interventions. Based on the growing number of positive research reports on mindfulness, you can more confidently assure your clients that mindfulness-based interventions are empirically supported.

SUMMARY

The brief history of mindfulness and important definitions discussed in this chapter laid the theoretical groundwork for mindfulness-based interventions discussed in upcoming chapters. I also reviewed important models of mindfulness that are being studied today, as well as some examples of research on the mechanisms of mindfulness. In the next chapter, I present in greater depth the benefits of mindfulness for various aspects of human functioning. I'll also take a closer look at how mindfulness influences cognitive functioning, emotion regulation, physical health, and interpersonal relationships.

chapter 2

Mindfulness Strategies and Benefits

The term "mindfulness strategies" refers to mindfulness responses that promote optimal human functioning. In this chapter, I organize these responses into several categories: cognitive and attentional, behavioral, emotional, and social. I'll describe these strategies and give examples of research evaluating their effects, and I'll outline many of the benefits of mindfulness and provide evidence-based support when available. Explaining these benefits to clients can increase their motivation to participate. In addition, knowing the benefits of mindfulness can help you evaluate whether your clients are profiting from mindfulness-based interventions. Benefits of mindfulness can serve as healthy outcomes in a mindfulness-based treatment plan, and you can study and document how and when these benefits occur because of the intervention.

UNDERSTANDING MINDFULNESS STRATEGIES

Mindfulness strategies are general responses that are influenced by mindfulness practice and in turn can enhance or decrease mindfulness. These strategies inform what types of techniques you might encourage clients to practice. For example, a client who has problems focusing when she's in challenging social situations might benefit from practicing the mountain meditation (described in full in chapter 4). In the mountain meditation, you instruct the client to sit quietly and notice her breathing. Then, after a few moments, you encourage her to bring to mind images about being a mountain. The mountain stands firm and unmoving through time. Though lightning may strike and set the trees on the mountain on fire, the mountain maintains its stillness. People may hike or build things on the mountain and rocks may tumble from the mountain's flanks, but the mountain itself remains solid and unmoving. Practicing this technique over time can help the client develop a feeling of inner strength and an understanding of the temporary nature of all things. This can help with emotion regulation in stressful social situations by providing a sense of solidness in the midst of interactions with others.

I label these strategies as cognitive and attentional, behavioral, emotional, and social because these concepts represent areas of human functioning that clients can control or influence. Certain mindfulness techniques can enhance some or all of these areas of functioning, a topic I'll discuss at length in chapter 3. Furthermore, research demonstrates that most people who increase their overall capacity for mindfulness tend to reap benefits in these areas of functioning (K. W. Brown et al., 2007a). For example, the client who learns the mountain meditation and improves her ability to regulate her emotions may then be able to more effectively pay attention in the moment. As a result, she will interact more positively with others, thereby improving her interpersonal relationships. Improving her interpersonal relationships may then enhance social functioning, resulting in perceptions of social support—a type of social strategy. Conversely, becoming less mindful in one area can influence a negative reaction in another area of functioning. For example, if a client becomes impatient in trying to reach a desired outcome such as improving her diet to achieve a healthier weight, she may become less open and generous with herself. She may become judgmental about her progress and get discouraged. Eventually, she may abandon her intention to eat a healthier diet, resulting in weight gain.

COGNITIVE AND ATTENTIONAL STRATEGIES

Cognitive and attentional strategies involve using mental abilities and skills to manipulate internal experiences such as thoughts, emotions, sensory perceptions, and images. The cognitive skills and abilities I'll discuss here are external versus internal cognitive focus, focused attention, metacognitive awareness, and observing. You can incorporate these cognitive and attentional strategies as you develop mindfulness-based interventions for your clients.

External vs. Internal Cognitive Focus

Mindfulness encourages attending to both internal and external stimuli in the present moment in a nonjudgmental and open manner. Some researchers suggest that paying attention to inner occurrences with acceptance leads to emotional benefits (Baer, 2006; Bishop et al., 2004). Paying attention to and accepting negative feelings and thoughts instead of avoiding them helps us work through these feelings and thoughts, and ultimately reduce them. Other researchers believe that attending mindfully to external events provides greater benefits than focusing inward (Herndon, 2008; K. W. Brown & Ryan, 2003). By being mindful of the external, we are able to more realistically negotiate current environmental stressors, leading to better outcomes. Mindfulness researchers are studying the relative benefits of an external versus internal focus of mindful attention (Herndon, 2008). It might be that the greatest cognitive benefit of mindfulness comes from increased flexibility in moving attention freely back and forth from internal to external focus.

Studies evaluating the relationship between neuroticism and mindfulness have provided support for the benefits of an external focus. Neuroticism is a personality trait characterized by a general tendency to experience negative feelings and irrational ideas and cope poorly with stress (Costa & McCrae, 1992). There is ample research evidence that people who score higher on neuroticism tend to have poorer health, more illness, and higher mortality rates compared to people who are less neurotic (Labbé & Fobes, 2010). Researchers have shown an inverse relationship between mindfulness and neuroticism, suggesting that people who tend to direct their attention internally ruminate on negative feelings and thoughts and avoid interacting with others. They are also more likely to score lower on measures of mindfulness. Felix Herndon (2008) reported on two studies where he measured mindfulness and found that it was correlated positively with attending to an external focus. He also found that higher levels of mindfulness and external encoding were associated with fewer cognitive errors. *External encoding* refers to making conclusions or decisions about the environment only when supported by sufficient data and external evidence. In contrast, *internal encoding* refers to making conclusions about the environment based more on expectations, which may lead to irrational conclusions about reality. External encoding may lead to better problem solving and improved ability to negotiate day-to-day living, resulting in lower levels of stress and depression.

Focused Attention

A considerable body of research demonstrates that mindfulness meditation training leads to improved focused attention, as well as higher levels of trait mindfulness (Zylowska, Smalley, & Schwartz, 2009). In chapter 1, I described several studies that demonstrated the positive effects of mindfulness training on attention (K. W. Brown & Ryan, 2003; K. W. Brown et al., 2007a). Remember, mindfulness denotes attention and awareness, and all of the different models of mindfulness emphasize the important role attention plays in being mindful. In mindfulness training, we are encouraged to attend in a certain way. At the bare minimum, we should attend with acceptance and nonjudgment. Attending mindfully increases accurate observation of internal and external experiences.

Research is needed to determine whether increased mindfulness improves memory, either short-term or long-term. A mindful person may be more likely to sustain focused attention long enough for information to be processed and stored by the brain. In addition, mindfulness may help improve retrieval of information by reducing distractions and allowing us to find stored memories more quickly.

Metacognitive Awareness

Mindfulness training improves our ability to think about our thoughts, feelings, and other internal experiences, a process known as *metacognitive awareness*. The ability to mentally step back and observe the inner workings of the mind can be helpful in many ways. First, it helps us develop the ability to observe thoughts, images, and affective experiences without identifying with them, an ability that mindfulness experts often refer to as *disidentification*. Disidentification facilitates a nonreactive stance toward feelings, thoughts, and images, resulting in less intense negative responses to irrelevant stimuli (Walsh & Shapiro, 2006). Second, metacognitive awareness allows us to widen our view of our current experience. By scanning thoughts and images, we may consider better ways to solve a problem, rather than responding impulsively to a particular experience. Another benefit of metacognitive awareness is that it can facilitate the experience of the temporary nature of all things, allowing us to let go of images, thoughts, or feelings that promote suffering.

Observing

Observing is a strategy based on metacognitive awareness. It's an element of Marsha Linehan's dialectical behavior therapy (1993), a mindfulness-based approach that has been used successfully for treatment of borderline personality disorder (Welch, Rizvi, & Dimidjian, 2006). Observing improves attention to current experiences and involves attending to experiences directly, without categorizing or conceptualizing in order to accept these experiences. Observing entails paying attention to sensory experiences without labeling them. In this way, we can enhance our skills in perceiving moment-to-moment experiences, both pleasant and unpleasant, without judging or avoiding these experiences. Thich Nhat Hanh (2000) tells a story of taking a walk with some children. One child asked him what the color of a tree was. He replied that it was the color of the tree. He responded this way to encourage the child to see the tree as it is, without labeling it with a particular color. Labeling things influences our experiences of them in the future and may limit our full experience of whatever we encounter.

BEHAVIORAL STRATEGIES

Mindfulness practice encourages spending some time each day sitting quietly, or at least slowing down while engaging in daily activities. Many clinicians using mindfulness-based interventions believe that daily meditation is the most effective and efficient way to develop mindfulness. Mindfulness-based stress reduction and mindfulness-based cognitive therapy both encourage daily meditation for the client as well as the therapist. Engaging in meditation and other mindfulness-based behaviors can have a variety of benefits, including reducing negative emotions and unhealthy behaviors and increasing focused attention and positive emotional states.

Clients with a variety of psychological or medical problems who are interested in reducing maladaptive behavior and improving their quality of life may benefit from mindfulness-based behavioral strategies. Engaging in meditation and other mindfulness-based behaviors can improve responses to negative emotions and decrease unhealthy and habitual behaviors. Acceptance of pain can lead to more adaptive behavior and a better quality of life. And engaging in behavior mindfully can increase focused attention and positive emotional states.

Exposure

Behavioral therapists have demonstrated that exposure to stimuli that are distressing to the client will lead to behavioral change (Sue & Sue, 2008). For example, the treatment of choice for specific phobias is exposure therapy. In exposure therapy, the therapist presents the client with the phobic stimulus and the client is not allowed to escape or avoid it. For example, a therapist guides a client across a bridge if that's what the client fears. Over time, the client will habituate to the stimulus and the conditioned phobic response will decline. The client will then be able to cross the bridge on her own when she comes to it.

Most clients are unwilling to interact directly with the phobic stimuli, so the next best treatment for phobias is systematic desensitization. In *systematic desensitization* the client first learns to relax. Once the client is relaxed, she's asked to imagine the phobic stimuli in a gradual way, using a hierarchy from least feared to most feared stimulus. If she becomes anxious, the therapist will ask her to relax. Once she's relaxed again, the process is repeated until the client can imagine the most feared stimulus and stay relaxed. When the client encounters the feared stimuli in real life, she will respond with relaxation instead of anxiety and be able to tolerate or interact with the previously feared stimuli.

Clinicians and researchers suggest that mindfulness can help change behavioral responses to the environment through the same mechanisms as systematic desensitization. In mindfulness meditation, clients are encouraged to allow all thoughts, images, and feelings into their awareness and observe them without judgment. Through exposure to these internal negative experiences in consciousness over time, the client will learn healthier ways to react to these stimuli in reality.

Supporting Behavioral Intentions

People often have strong intentions to engage in healthier behaviors but frequently fail to act on these intentions (Chatzisarantis & Hagger, 2007). Failure to inhibit unhealthy behaviors and substitute healthy behaviors can perpetuate health problems. Many factors can influence people's intentions to change their behavior, including peer pressure, ability to successfully control the behavior, and negative and positive attitudes regarding the intended behavior. Mindfulness models predict that the intention to attend using the mindfulness qualities should increase the likelihood that positive behavior change will occur. A study that supports this hypothesis measured observed habits and other psychological variables, including mindfulness of physical activity (Chatzisarantis & Hagger, 2007). Results indicated that the effects of mindfulness were independent of effects observed for habit and other psychosocial variables in predicting physical activity. The researchers concluded that participants acting habitually and not mindfully were less likely to act on physical activity intentions than those who reported acting mindfully and not habitually.

Mindfulness can help reduce impulsiveness and unhealthy automatic or habitual behaviors by promoting greater awareness of potential adaptive responses to events (K. W. Brown et al., 2007a, 2007b). Several studies support the idea that mindfulness can facilitate more adaptive behavioral responses. In an example of these types of studies, researchers reported that trait mindfulness was correlated with higher levels of self-control (Tangney, Baumeister, & Boone, 2004). Self-control can be adaptive and facilitate the development of healthy habits.

Another example of using mindfulness to reduce impulsiveness is a mindfulness-based intervention for binge-eating behavior (Kristeller, Baer, & Quillian-Wolever, 2006). Mindfulness meditation is used to help clients become aware of automatic patterns of responding, particularly to food. The focus is on helping clients become aware of hunger and satiety cues based on physiological need, rather than emotions or thoughts that trigger eating. A few studies have been reported that indicate decreases in binge eating in participants who engaged in eating-related meditations (Kristeller et al., 2006; Wolever & Best, 2009).

Embracing Pain

When people develop chronic pain, they typically experience significant decreases in quality of life and activity. Mindfulness-based interventions for pain focus on helping clients improve their quality of life, including engaging in physical activity and reducing pain-related behaviors, such as taking pain medications (Dahl & Lundgren, 2006). Unlike other approaches to pain management, including cognitive behavioral approaches, the treatment goal in mindfulness-based interventions isn't a reduction in pain. Instead, clients are encouraged to attend to pain sensations using mindfulness qualities, particularly acceptance. They are taught that pain is one of many states of human experience and that struggling to escape the pain causes more suffering. In some respects, the level of the pain experience is dependent on the client's attachment to thoughts, images, and feelings of pain. When clients are attached to these experiences, they generally attempt to escape the pain through a variety of pain-related behaviors, including avoiding activities they believe will increase the pain. Through mindfulness training, these clients can learn to engage in adaptive behaviors even in the presence of pain and suffering. More research is being reported supporting the idea that this can reduce pain-related behaviors, improve quality of life, and even reduce the experience of pain (Dahl & Lundgren, 2006).

EMOTIONAL STRATEGIES

As mentioned in the introduction, trait mindfulness, or dispositional mindfulness, is a person's general tendency to be mindful. A growing body of research indicates that trait mindfulness is positively correlated with healthy emotional functioning and negatively correlated with emotional distress and psychopathology. People who participate in mindfulness-based interventions tend to experience decreases in negative emotional functioning and increases in positive emotions, such as happiness, relaxation, and peacefulness. Research studies report decreases in anxiety, depression, eating disorders, substance abuse, and other types of psychopathology among those who practice mindfulness (Coffey & Hartman, 2008). Although there is research support for the beneficial effects of mindfulness on emotional functioning, most studies haven't focused on the mechanisms involved in producing these emotional benefits.

For some clients and some types of problems, either the clients are not able to identify irrational beliefs, or they become so overwhelmed by their emotions that they can't think clearly or accept a more rational view of their experiences. With these clients, you may find that a mindfulness-based intervention is the key to helping them regulate their emotions more effectively. Improving emotion regulation, fostering positive emotional states, and helping clients not overidentify with their feelings are important mindfulness strategies for reducing the symptoms of most psychological disorders.

Improving Emotion Regulation

Mindfulness may help regulate emotional functioning by means of the cognitive and attentional strategies described above, which could help people recognize distressing thoughts and that these thoughts don't represent reality (Coffey & Hartman, 2008). In one study that provides support for this mechanism, participants engaged in one of three experimental conditions for fifteen minutes: a mindfulness-based breathing exercise, an unfocused attention exercise, or a worry-inducing exercise (Arch & Craske, 2006). Participants first completed measures of mindfulness and emotional functioning. After the groups participated in one of the three exercises, they were exposed to highly negative pictures. Those in the mindfulness-based breathing group were more willing to view the pictures and reported less negative affect than participants in the unfocused attention or worry groups. The researchers concluded that their study provides support for the emotion regulation function of mindfulness. In another randomized controlled trial, clients with generalized anxiety disorder were assigned to either a mindfulness-based treatment group or a waiting list control group (Roemer, Orsillo, & Salters-Pedneault, 2008). At the end of treatment and at three- and nine-month follow-ups, anxiety symptoms were significantly lower among the mindfulness-based treatment group compared to the control group. The researchers also found that the treatment group demonstrated decreases in experiential avoidance and increases in mindfulness. This supports the effectiveness of incorporating mindfulness-based strategies when developing treatment protocols for reducing avoidance of negative emotional states.

Fostering Positive Emotional States

Affective qualities of mindfulness include gratitude, gentleness, generosity, empathy, and loving-kindness. These emotional responses may result from the intention to attend with mindfulness. Furthermore, these emotional responses can be intentionally nurtured through meditation practices like loving-kindness meditation or attending with gratitude to experiences throughout the day. Clients can be encouraged to linger with positive emotions by paying attention to them and savoring feelings of generosity, gentleness, and kindness. It is important to note that fostering positive emotions is not the same thing as becoming attached to them. Becoming attached to good feelings can eventually lead to suffering as the person avoids negative emotions or reality in order to hold on to positive emotions. So being in the moment with and appreciating positive emotions can foster joy, if tempered by the realization that holding too tightly to these affirmative feelings can lead to mindlessness. Dan Clendenin (2002) elegantly summarizes this point in one of his weekly essays on his website: "A life of gratitude accepts the bad with the good. Genuine gratitude is not a zero-sum game in which thankfulness increases the more fortunate you are and decreases the more adversity you experience."

Though research on this topic is limited, there have been some studies that can help us understand the relationship between the affective qualities of mindfulness and better emotion regulation. Mindfulness can reduce negative emotional states through the practice of nonattachment (K. W. Brown et al., 2007a). Remember that nonattachment involves a conscious decision to let go of, or at least reduce, one's grip on thoughts, feelings, images, or other experiences. Developing nonattachment can reduce rumination. Excessive and chronic rumination can lead to anxiety, stress, depression, and a variety of disordered emotions and behaviors. A recent study compared a mindfulness meditation training program to a somatic relaxation training program and to a control group (Jain et al., 2007). Somatic relaxation training included autogenic training, progressive relaxation training, simple breathing techniques, and imagery techniques with the goal of producing relaxation. This randomized controlled trial demonstrated that both mindfulness meditation and somatic relaxation training resulted in reduced psychological distress compared to the control group. However, reduction in psychological distress for the mindfulness meditation group was mediated by greater reductions in rumination and distraction compared to the somatic relaxation and the control groups. The meditation training also produced greater levels of positive states than the relaxation training.

Another study reported an inverse relationship between mindfulness and negative emotional functioning (Coffey & Hartman, 2008). Participants completed measures of trait mindfulness, emotion regulation, nonattachment, rumination, and psychological distress. The researchers evaluated the relationship between mindfulness and psychological distress and found that emotion regulation, nonattachment, and rumination all played a significant role in the relationship between mindfulness and distress. These studies support the approach of incorporating mindfulness-based techniques into interventions to help reduce rumination and promote better emotion regulation.

Developing Nonattachment to Emotions

Mindfulness improves emotion regulation and helps reduce negative emotional states and clinical levels of emotional distress. Mindfulness practice encourages embracing suffering and negative emotions by observing but not overidentifying with these emotions. This helps clients experience the temporary nature of their negative feelings and begin to understand the benefits of not trying to avoid or rationalize their emotions.

In helping clients cope with negative feelings, mindfulness is quite different than using a cognitive behavioral therapy approach. A CBT approach focuses on reducing negative emotions by encouraging clients to identify the irrational beliefs that produce these feelings. For many clients this approach can be successful, as indicated by the research supporting CBT as an effective treatment for depression. However, research has shown that mindfulness-based cognitive therapy (MBCT) might be a better treatment choice than CBT for preventing recurrence of depressive episodes (Coffman, Dimidjian, & Baer, 2006). MBCT helps clients nonjudgmentally observe temporary feelings of sadness and depression, which are often a trigger for relapse of major depression. Clients trained in mindfulness are less likely to ruminate on temporary or even normal feelings of sadness, thus helping prevent relapse. This research comparing CBT with MBCT is a good example of using an evidence-based approach to determine the best intervention for helping people change.

SOCIAL STRATEGIES

Mindfulness fosters a greater awareness of being a whole system within multiple levels of other systems. Recall the intentional systemic mindfulness model, which proposes that mindfulness develops feelings of interconnectedness with others. Although clinical observations support the notion that people who engage in mindfulness-based practices report feelings of greater connectedness to others, there isn't much empirical research to support this claim. There has been some research evaluating the effects of mindfulness on improving therapists' and health practitioners' mental health, suggesting that this can improve their relationships with clients, as well as client outcomes (Shapiro & Carlson, 2009). Other studies have evaluated how mindfulness can enhance romantic relationships (Barnes, Brown, Krusemarck, Campbell, & Rogge, 2007). More research is needed to evaluate the role of mindfulness in increasing perceptions of social support and enhancing social relationships.

Communicating Mindfully

Mindfulness practice facilitates the ability to focus on others more clearly. It helps develop listening skills that allow a person to accurately hear what other people are saying. Interestingly, therapists are being trained in mindfulness to improve their ability to empathize with and relate to their clients. Research is beginning to demonstrate that therapists who are trained in mindfulness may have better results with their clients than therapists who don't receive such training (Schure, Christopher, & Christopher, 2008). These benefits may be due to increased therapist empathy and decreased therapist stress and burnout.

Increasing Empathy

Practicing mindfulness may increase the ability to empathize more accurately with others. In one study (Schure et al., 2008), counseling students who were trained in mindfulness reported increases in feelings of empathy toward their clients' suffering. The students attributed this to being able to focus on the present moment with their clients instead of noticing their own anxiety or trying to figure out how to help their clients. Higher levels of therapist empathy have been associated with better treatment outcomes and are considered an important factor in all therapy approaches (Sue & Sue, 2008).

In a prospective cohort-controlled study, therapists in training received either mindfulness-based stress reduction plus clinical training as usual, or just clinical training as usual (Shapiro, Brown, & Biegel, 2007). Compared to participants in the control group, those who received MBSR reported significant increases in self-compassion and positive affect and decreases in rumination, negative affect, and state and trait anxiety. The researchers propose that learning to reduce stress and increase positive coping skills can help reduce therapist burnout. Mindfulness-based skills may also help therapists in training provide better quality therapy to their clients.

One study found no relationship between level of trait mindfulness of therapists in training and clients' reports of treatment outcome (Stanley et al., 2006). However, this study measured trait mindfulness and assessed the effectiveness of treatment outcomes for manualized treatments, which require the therapist to rigidly follow the treatment protocol. This study found that therapists lower in trait mindfulness reported greater improvements in their clients than therapists with higher trait mindfulness did. The researchers conclude that higher levels of therapist mindfulness may reduce the effects of manualized treatments, as this trait may cause therapists to focus more on the moment-to-moment occurrences in the therapeutic experience and, as a result, not attend as well to the treatment protocol. The researchers didn't measure therapists' adherence to the manual, so their argument isn't based on adherence data. Another interpretation of the results of this study is that therapists with lower trait mindfulness may not attend as closely to clients' symptoms at the end of treatment compared to therapists with higher trait mindfulness. Also, clients who don't feel listened to may not open up to their therapist as much and therefore may be less likely to fully share their concerns with their therapist (Hubble, Duncan, & Miller, 1999). Another issue with this study and those discussed above is that the participants were all therapists in training.

Two other studies evaluated client outcomes with therapists in training who practiced Zen meditation. The first, a nonrandomized, sequential, cohort pilot study, found that patients of therapists who meditated reported better progress in changing their behavior (Grepmair, Mitterlehner, Loew, & Nickel, 2007). The second study (Grepmair, Mitterlehner, Loew, Bachler, et al., 2007) utilized a similar approach but used a randomized controlled design. Therapists in training were randomly assigned to learn Zen meditation or be in the control group. Both groups were trained in therapy as usual. Patients didn't know whether their therapists practiced meditation. The patients of the therapists who were meditating reported increased understanding of their own psychodynamics and improvement in their symptoms compared to patients of therapists in the control group.

It would be interesting to see the results of studies that evaluate the effectiveness of expert therapists who employ evidence-based interventions. Of particular interest would be examining therapist mindfulness and client outcomes for therapists who use MBSR and MBCT with clients, as these mindfulness-based approaches require or encourage therapists to develop their own mindfulness practice. Another concern with studies evaluating therapist mindfulness and treatment outcomes is that they all use the Mindful Attention Awareness Scale (MAAS). Although this is a relatively valid measure of trait mindfulness, it's limited in that it measures only moment-to-moment awareness.

Newer measures of mindfulness, like the Five Facet Mindfulness Questionnaire (FFMQ), assess other dimensions of mindfulness that might be important for therapist effectiveness. For example, the FFMQ measures awareness, nonjudging, nonreactivity, describing, and observing. I hope that more studies will examine client outcomes of therapists who are trained in mindfulness-based interventions compared to those who are not, using a more comprehensive measure of mindfulness, such as the FFMQ. In addition, it would be interesting to compare the effectiveness of therapists lower in trait mindfulness versus those with higher trait mindfulness.

Enhancing Romantic Relationships

The positive effects of mindfulness on romantic relationships may be due to several factors, including fostering patience with others. This mindfulness quality encourages people to respond thoughtfully to their partner in negative social situations. Preliminary research suggests that mindfulness might promote better communication and higher quality of romantic relationships (K. W. Brown et al. 2007a). A recent study found that higher levels of trait mindfulness were predictive of relationship satisfaction among dating couples (Barnes et al., 2007). In addition, higher levels of mindfulness were related to greater ability to effectively respond to stressful interactions between partners. The researchers also evaluated the role of mindfulness when couples were in the midst of a relationship conflict. Higher trait mindfulness scores predicted less anxiety and anger when in a relationship conflict than lower scores did. The lower negative emotional responses to the conflict were associated with lower preconflict negative emotional states.

Kirk Brown and Shari Cordon (2009) suggest that mindfulness plays a preventive role in reducing negative emotional states in response to relationship conflicts. They propose that the more mindful people are when entering a stressful situation, the more likely it is that they will respond positively in their perception of their partner and the relationship. Cultivating mindfulness can improve social relationships by helping people develop better emotion regulation in demanding social situations. It's also likely that mindfulness promotes greater openness to and acceptance of others' negative feelings and thoughts or differing perceptions of the problem at hand.

SUMMARY

In this chapter I have reviewed mindfulness strategies and provided examples of research studies evaluating the effectiveness of these strategies. I described potential benefits of mindfulness practice and, when available, presented research on these claims. You can use this information to help motivate clients, and also to determine appropriate treatment outcomes when using mindfulness-based interventions with clients. The next chapter builds on this by addressing practical considerations in bringing mindfulness-based interventions into your clinical practice.

chapter 3

Practical Considerations in Using Mindfulness Techniques with Clients

Before selecting specific mindfulness techniques, you must consider the overall intervention plan for any given client. The more clients are able to engage their attention with the intention of embodying mindfulness qualities, the more they'll grow in their capacity to be mindful. You should introduce the mindfulness techniques in chapters 4 and 5 with patience and a nonstriving attitude, and encourage clients to explore gently and with curiosity the experiences they encounter when using these techniques. You can suggest to clients that these techniques are not something to "master"; rather, they offer a new and freeing way to experience internal and external occurrences. This allows clients to approach mindfulness practices without a desire to achieve "success" or do them "right."

Mindfulness techniques will help your clients become attentive to their experiences in the here and now. Sometimes paying attention in the moment can be uncomfortable, even painful. At other times, it can provide experiences of relaxation, peace, happiness, and joy. At yet other times, it may lead to experiences that are a mixture of positive and negative emotions and thoughts. If you observe clients striving for a particular experience, you might want to give gentle feedback, encouraging them to let go of these expectations.

All of the techniques I'll present in this book involve mindfully focusing attention onto certain experiences, thoughts, or feelings. Mindfulness techniques can be *formal*, meaning they're practiced at a certain time and place with specific instructions, such as certain types of meditation. Or they can be *informal*, meaning they can be practiced throughout the day, such as mindful eating or noticing your breath before you answer the phone. When reviewing the literature on mindfulness, I found that most writers suggest that the capacity to be mindful improves with increased practice of both formal and informal techniques. Most mindfulness-based interventions use a combination of techniques for clients, some in session with the therapist, and some assigned as "homework," in which clients are given exercises to practice and encouraged to keep a journal of their practice experiences or a simple record of their homework. You can then review the client's homework experience in the next session. You should review these experiences with the client with curiosity and acceptance, in a nonjudging way. Depending on the client and his experiences, you may encourage him to continue practicing the same technique in the same way, or you may suggest spending more time on the practice or an alternative exercise.

Mindfulness-based approaches are often presented in a group format. Later in this chapter I present information on how to develop a group approach. All of the mindfulness techniques in this book can be readily incorporated into individual therapy as well.

DIFFERENT MINDFULNESS TECHNIQUES FOR DIFFERENT PROBLEMS

Research on how effectively and extensively specific mindfulness techniques increase a person's capacity to be mindful is growing, but we still don't know enough to make confident conclusions based on empirical evidence. Mindfulness-based interventions incorporate different formal and informal techniques and practice schedules based on what the clinician thinks is most beneficial for the client and the problem the intervention is designed to address. However, research is needed to identify whether certain techniques are actually more beneficial than others for particular populations or problems.

For a clear example of how mindfulness techniques vary in different interventions, consider mindfulness-based stress reduction for coping with chronic illness or pain, versus dialectical behavior therapy for clients with borderline personality disorder (Linehan, 1993). MBSR incorporates sitting and walking meditation, the body scan, yoga, and moment-to-moment awareness for helping clients cope with illness or pain. In MBSR, participants are encouraged to engage in sitting meditation, the body scan, or yoga for at least forty-five minutes a day. MBSR participants also attend a daylong mindfulness retreat that includes practicing meditation, the body scan, and other mindfulness techniques in a group setting. DBT doesn't require clients to practice daily meditation. Instead, they're taught to attend mindfully to day-to-day activities.

Comparing MBSR to DBT illustrates that different mindfulness techniques and approaches are used for different populations and problems. Although DBT makes use of mindfulness, providing greater detail on DBT is beyond the scope of this book, as it combines mindfulness with other approaches. For more information on DBT, see Marsha Linehan's writings on the subject (Linehan, 1993). In chapter 9, I will outline more specifically which mindfulness techniques (or adaptations of them) might be more effective for specific problems from an evidence-based perspective.

DIFFERENT TYPES OF MINDFULNESS TECHNIQUES

I've grouped mindfulness techniques into two categories: formal and informal mindfulness practices. In the next two chapters, details are provided on how to teach these techniques to clients. Within each category, I'll describe the more common evidence-based techniques currently included in mindfulness-based interventions. This chapter provides information on when and how to integrate these mindfulness techniques into your work with your clients. I discuss general concerns and issues that clients may have regarding mindfulness-based interventions. Later in the book more specific information on how to formulate treatment plans for your clients using mindfulness-based techniques is presented. I'll also show you how to empirically assess your clients' progress in developing mindfulness, as well as their improvement in problem areas.

INTRODUCING MINDFULNESS TO CLIENTS

You can introduce the idea of mindfulness techniques when developing the initial treatment plan with your client. It's best to discuss the concept of mindfulness as described in chapter 1: the intention to pay attention, moment by moment, to inner and outer experiences with the qualities of acceptance, nonjudging, nonstriving, patience, trust, openness, and letting go.

Explaining the Benefits of Mindfulness Techniques

To help clients see the benefits of practicing mindfulness, you can describe the mindfulness qualities and discuss how mindfulness practice fosters these qualities and can help reduce the problems they are experiencing. You can also point out that mindfulness has been shown to be effective for many health and psychological disorders. If need be, refer back to chapter 2, where I outlined the benefits of mindfulness, so that you can focus on those most clearly related to your client's concerns.

For example, if a client has anxiety problems you can address his particular issues by reviewing the cognitive, behavioral, and emotional benefits discussed in chapter 2. You can tell the client that mindfulness will enhance his ability to cope with anxiety-producing events through the promotion of moment-by-moment awareness. Breathing and meditation techniques from chapter 4 and yoga and other informal practices from chapter 5 can be used in conjunction with other therapeutic techniques to help the client cope with anxiety and become more aware of other emotions.

I included yoga with informal practices because, although it involves breathing mindfully, it requires the client to move about and focus on the body instead of being still. Also, yoga postures can be incorporated into daily activities such as before and after exercise, sitting at the desk, or waiting in line. Yoga can be practiced to ready the body for meditation, as it allows the person to connect to, strengthen, and relax the body to prepare for long periods of formal sitting meditation.

Addressing Concerns About Mindfulness

There are some common questions and fears that might come up for clients. Address the time commitment involved in practicing mindfulness techniques on a daily basis up front. Clients who are unwilling to devote forty-five minutes to an hour for the first few weeks of the intervention may not reap the full benefits of mindfulness practice. In chapter 8, I suggest some time adaptations for different mindfulness exercises that might be helpful for clients who are unable to commit this much time to daily practice.

Clients may express that they dislike or are unable to engage in some of the mindfulness techniques. For example, clients with a chronic pain condition or illness may express anxiety about engaging in movement exercises or about sitting or lying down for long periods when practicing some of the meditation techniques. Even clients who don't suffer from pain or illness may complain about discomfort or physical limitations.

Clients may be self-conscious, believe that they can't do a particular practice, or have difficulty with falling asleep during the exercise. It's important to address these concerns as they arise. Depending on the issue, you can tell clients to be open and patient toward what they are struggling with. Recommend that they give the practice a little time and observe the discomfort (pain, anxiety, boredom, and so on) instead of reacting to it. Often, this approach allows clients to experience a subsiding of the discomfort or to find that they can do the practice if they are patient with themselves.

On the other hand, some concerns may need to be addressed immediately, such as not being able to sit to meditate. If this is the case, you can help clients adapt the technique or choose another practice. In chapter 8, I provide information on how to adapt mindfulness techniques for special populations.

Though it doesn't come up often, some people might be concerned because of the idea that mindfulness comes from Buddhism. You can explain to such clients that although mindfulness has its roots in Buddhism, it is considered a secular practice and not tied to any specific religious faith or community. You can encourage clients to talk about this concern with their minister or other spiritual advisor before committing to a mindfulness-based approach.

Assessing Client Readiness for a Mindfulness-Based Intervention

You can begin introducing clients to mindfulness techniques after you've outlined the commitment involved and the benefits of practicing mindfulness and have addressed any concerns they may have. If clients agree to engage in mindfulness practice, consult chapter 7 for details on how to formulate plans for using particular techniques. You can use the suggested protocols in chapters 8 and 9 to determine when and how to do so.

It can be helpful to get a sense of how motivated clients may be to change. In my work with clients, I administer the Outcome Rating Scale (ORS), developed by Scott Miller and colleagues (Miller, Duncan, Brown, Sparks, & Claud, 2003). Scores on the ORS can give you information on clients' overall functioning. Clients who score high on this scale often aren't motivated to change. You can give the ORS at the beginning of each session to determine whether clients are improving. Miller (2009) found that clients whose scores don't improve by the sixth session tend to either drop out of therapy, worsen, or continue in therapy with no improvement.

GUIDES TO PRACTICE

The mindfulness techniques described in chapters 4 and 5 are drawn from many books, research studies, and my own clinical and personal experiences with mindfulness. You can refer to the resources section at the end of the book as well as the references list if you're interested in learning more about these techniques. From my own experience in conducting mindfulness-based interventions, I believe it is important for the therapist to have a personal mindfulness practice. I will discuss how to develop one in chapter 10. As you develop your own mindfulness practice and teach these techniques to clients, you'll probably find yourself varying the instructions and content. This is fine. None of the practices is set in stone. In fact, new techniques and new versions of these classic mindfulness techniques are always being developed.

Mindfulness techniques should be used in an open and flexible manner. If you read about these techniques in other books, you'll see minor and sometimes significant differences from one author to another in how they are described. I have been influenced most by master teachers Thich Nhat Hanh, Jon Kabat-Zinn, and Jack Kornfield in my understanding of these techniques for myself and in teaching my clients and students. As you read about the techniques, you may notice that the descriptions are very close to the instructions you've heard on recordings by these master teachers of mindfulness. I've tried to blend different versions of these instructions in providing examples of how to apply these techniques. Most research on mindfulness-based interventions, particularly mindfulness-based stress reduction and mindfulness-based cognitive therapy, use instructions set forth by Jon Kabat-Zinn in *Full Catastrophe Living* (1990).

RECORDING MINDFULNESS TECHNIQUES

Many recordings of mindfulness techniques by these master teachers of mindfulness, and others, are available for purchase. Listening to these recordings can help you develop the proper rhythm and timing for these exercises. If you're leading the exercise, use a quiet and warm voice and take your time in setting forth the instructions or reading through the script. You can also find written versions of these instructions in various sources, particularly the appendices of recent books on mindfulness-based interventions. I will also provide basic scripts for these exercises in chapters 4 and 5. You can encourage clients to make their own audio recordings of the exercise instructions to use in their mindfulness practice.

Guided meditation can be helpful at all levels of mindfulness practice. In time, you and your clients will be able to practice these techniques without guidance. However, it might be helpful to listen to guided meditations periodically to learn new techniques or to remind yourself of aspects that could be helpful for you and your clients.

THE PRACTICE ENVIRONMENT

The environment in which clients practice will influence their experience when engaging in mindfulness techniques. Generally, new ideas and techniques are introduced in the therapist's office. Then the client is encouraged to practice at home or in other real-life environments, such as at work or school. In-office practice allows you to discuss with clients in detail the reasons for engaging in a specific technique. It also gives the client a chance to try it out. Then you can discuss potential obstacles the client may encounter when practicing in real-life environments. This is a good start, but home practice is the key in ensuring that clients establish a daily routine of formal mindfulness practice and integrate mindfulness into their everyday life.

The Therapy Environment

Although it is important to provide a comfortable and clean space where your clients can practice mindfulness, it is also important for clients to learn how to practice even with discomfort and distractions. That said, the therapy environment should be quiet and offer the client a variety of options for sitting and lying down. Sitting options should include a comfortable and clean space on the floor, a bench, or chairs for sitting meditation. You can provide a *zafu* (a meditation cushion) for clients who want to sit on the floor. For lying down, you can provide floor mats or reclining chairs. Monitor the room temperature and ask if the client is comfortable; if not, adjust accordingly. Ask your staff to not interrupt sessions or forward calls to your therapy room. If you are in a noisy environment, you might consider using a white noise machine to buffer these sounds.

The Environment for At-Home Practice

Clients who aren't familiar with mindfulness techniques should be encouraged to find quiet and comfortable places to practice so they won't be distracted by the environment or disturbed by others. Instruct clients to turn off the phone and let others in the house know that they aren't available during the practice. If clients practice at work, they should find a quiet place to be and ask others not to disturb them. As clients develop expertise in using mindfulness techniques, they will be better able to observe distractions without responding to them in a negative manner. Even so, experts on mindfulness think it's important to spend some time each day practicing mindfulness in a quiet and distraction-free environment.

GROUP FORMAT

All of the exercises in chapters 4 and 5 can be done in individual or group format. Your clients will benefit from experiencing both settings when learning how to practice mindfulness. A group format can encourage feelings of support from others and strengthens the sense of interconnectedness with all beings. Generally, group exercises are conducted in silence, but this format can include a discussion period after engaging in an exercise to allow group members to process and share their experiences with each other. Participants may find comfort in hearing other group members' struggles and successes. They might also get new ideas from each other on how to foster mindfulness.

Mindfulness-based stress reduction is usually conducted in a group format. Many of the mindfulness-based programs being developed are carried out completely in group format. Groups are more efficient than individual interventions in terms of both cost and time. Only minimal research has been done comparing the effectiveness of group versus individual mindfulness-based interventions. It would be useful to have evidence-based data to help clinicians select which clients might benefit more from one format or the other. For now, you can use criteria from group and systems studies to help determine which individuals might do better in group versus individual psychotherapy. A discussion of group processes is beyond the scope of this book.

Mindfulness-based interventions have been reported to be successful with small and very large groups of participants. A good number of studies evaluating mindfulness-based interventions for a variety of disorders and problems use group formats when delivering these interventions (Baer, 2006). These studies report group approaches to be successful for stress reduction, eating disorders, prevention of depression relapse, chronic illness and pain, and anxiety disorders.

You might consider using a group format if you've identified at least six clients with similar problems or desired outcomes. You should screen your clients to make sure they would be suitable for a group experience. Clients who are actively psychotic or hostile may not be good candidates for group intervention. To present the idea of a group intervention as a benefit to your clients, point out that it's cost-effective and that the experience provides opportunities to learn from others.

MINDFULNESS-BASED RETREATS

Mindfulness-based retreats are generally conducted in a group format. These retreats can be just one day long or last for days or even weeks. Successful retreats take careful planning. They generally involve more than one leader of mindfulness practices, as well as support staff. Activities should move smoothly from one to the next, and enough space should be provided for participants to feel comfortable.

In mindfulness-based stress reduction, clients are asked to attend a daylong mindfulness retreat, usually toward the end of the eight-week intervention program. These retreats may include a large number of participants. Most of the mindfulness techniques described in chapters 4 and 5 are practiced throughout the day, including eating lunch mindfully. Many of the mindfulness-based interventions being developed include at least one all-day session, usually at the end of the program. Some programs offer periodic full-day retreats for clients who have completed a program and want a booster session or want to deepen their mindfulness practice. In chapters 8 and 9, I discuss when a mindfulness retreat should be included in programs for particular populations and problems.

Multiday retreats are usually conducted mostly in silence. They can involve all of the different types of exercises described in chapters 4 and 5. These retreats might include some individual consultation time with the leaders of the retreat and some time for lectures and group discussion. Retreats often include lodging and meals so that participants can focus completely on developing their mindfulness. Retreats should be conducted in environments that provide lots of individual space and the opportunity to explore nature.

Regardless of length, retreats can be focused on certain populations or people with particular problems, but they can also be open to anyone who wants to learn more about mindfulness and how to practice it. Retreats are also used to train professionals who plan to conduct individual or group mindfulness-based interventions. Retreats for therapists can help them enhance their understanding of mindfulness or learn new mindfulness techniques.

Retreats can be helpful for a variety of problems, including stress, anxiety, depression, chronic pain and illness, eating disorders, and marital problems. There isn't much research available to determine what type or length of retreat might be most effective for particular populations or problems. Most of the studies thus far have used a one-day retreat that was mostly a silent retreat.

If you can't provide a mindfulness-based retreat experience for your clients, there may be retreats available in your area to which you can refer them. You might explore prescribing a solitary at-home retreat for some clients, but this won't provide the potential benefits of the group experience. Keep in mind that most church- or other community-conducted retreats aren't focused on mindfulness. Unless you're certain that a retreat is primarily mindfulness based, you shouldn't recommend it to clients as an extension of a mindfulness-based intervention. If a client asks about participating in a retreat that isn't mindfulness based, explore with him the type of retreat, the possible outcomes and benefits of the retreat, and the client's desired outcomes. Even if a retreat isn't mindfulness based, it might be beneficial for the client if it produces his desired outcomes. However, if the type of retreat and the potential outcomes seem counter to the work the client is doing with you, recommend against participating at this time.

SUMMARY

In this chapter, I outlined general principles for introducing mindfulness techniques to your clients. An advantage of using a mindfulness-based approach to helping people change is that it provides structure and flexibility at the same time. The structure involves a variety of mindfulness techniques that have been proven effective for a wide variety of problems. The flexibility comes from the very nature of mindfulness. A mindfulness-based intervention is carried out using the mindfulness qualities of acceptance, nonjudging, nonstriving, patience, trust, openness, and letting go. As you introduce each mindfulness technique or strategy to clients, you can highlight these qualities and encourage clients to approach each technique with these qualities as well.

In the next two chapters I present the basic formal and informal mindfulness techniques used in most mindfulness-based programs. In addition to describing each technique, I provide details on how to guide clients through the exercise. Where relevant, I also discuss research support for the effectiveness of specific techniques.

chapter 4

Mindfulness Techniques for Formal Practice

I have grouped mindfulness practices into two categories: formal practice, covered in this chapter, and informal practice, covered in chapter 5. Within each category, I describe the more common mindfulness techniques currently studied and used in mindfulness-based interventions. I also discuss research evidence supporting the effectiveness of specific techniques.

There are many types of formal practice that can be used in mindfulness-based interventions. All could be considered forms of meditation. These include but are not limited to breathing exercises, the body scan, various sitting meditations, loving-kindness meditation, and walking meditation. As noted in earlier chapters, research suggests that developing a meditation practice can lead to many positive changes, including improved emotional coping, healthier physiological functioning, and changes in brain structure and functions (Treadway & Lazar, 2009).

OBSERVING THE BREATH

All mindfulness-based interventions include some type of instruction on how to use breathing to foster mindfulness. Mindfulness-based stress reduction and mindfulness-based cognitive therapy both encourage paying attention to the breath right from the outset. You can instruct your clients to notice their breathing and to gently bring their attention back to the breath whenever it wanders. In the following simple breathing exercise, you aren't asking clients to change anything; you're just asking them to notice the breath. The very act of noticing the breath will pull them into the present moment.

Instructions for Observing the Breath

Therapist: When you find yourself dwelling on negative thoughts or feelings, you can use your breath to bring yourself back to the moment. Simply notice the air entering your nostrils and feel your chest and abdomen moving to bring air into your lungs and body. Go ahead and try it now. You can close or lower your eyelids, whichever you prefer. Notice the breath coming into your nose, traveling into your lungs, and then going out again. Don't try to change your breathing. Just take notice of your breath moment by moment.

Allow the client to take about ten breaths, reminding her to just notice her breath. Then ask her how this practice felt. You can also take this opportunity to educate the client on the benefits of the practice.

Therapist: Okay, how did that feel?

Client: I feel more relaxed.

Therapist: Often just pausing for a few moments throughout the day can help you get in touch with your body and whatever is present in your life in that moment. By noticing your breath, you can remember to let go of thoughts about the past and future and relax into the moment.

DIAPHRAGMATIC BREATHING

For some of the meditation exercises, you'll instruct your client to do slow, deep breathing as part of the practice. In MBSR, clients are instructed on diaphragmatic breathing (Kabat-Zinn, 2005). This technique involves breathing deeply and using the diaphragm muscle to push air out of the lungs when exhaling and to expand the lungs when breathing in. When stressed, people often hold their breath or breathe rapidly and shallowly, from the top of their chest. Rapid breathing can cause people to take in too much oxygen, resulting in feeling light-headed or having tingling in the extremities. This increases sympathetic nervous system arousal, which can heighten physiological and emotional stress reactions. Slow diaphragmatic breathing, on the other hand, can have a calming effect by stimulating the parasympathetic nervous system, which slows the heart rate and counters other physiological and emotional stress reactions.

In MBSR, the goal of diaphragmatic breathing is to help people focus attention on the present moment using the mindfulness qualities. As a side benefit, people often feel more relaxed if they take the time to stop and breathe mindfully. Initially, ask clients to spend ten to fifteen minutes a day focusing on their breath and breathing slowly and deeply. Encourage them to find a quiet spot where they can sit or lie down in a comfortable position and practice diaphragmatic breathing. For many people, this can be a challenging task for even just a few minutes.

Instructions for Diaphragmatic Breathing

Therapist: Sometimes it can be helpful not only to notice your breath, but to slow it down and make it deeper. This is called diaphragmatic breathing, and it can help you calm down and relax a bit. Let me explain how to do it.

Sit in a relaxed position. Place one hand on your abdomen and the other at the top of your chest. Now notice the air coming into your nostrils and down into your chest and abdomen. If you can't feel your chest or abdomen moving, you might want to think of breathing in more deeply. If you begin to feel light-headed or experience tingling in your lips or fingertips during this practice, you're probably breathing too rapidly. If that happens, stop, breathe naturally, and wait until you feel better before trying again.

Now follow my voice. I'll ask you to breathe in slowly, then pause, then breathe out slowly, then pause. Let's try it. Breathe in. *(Count to five in your head.)* Now pause for three seconds *(pause)*, then slowly breathe out. *(Count to five in your head.)* Now pause. Breathe in again... *(Guide the client through ten breaths.)* How did that feel?

Explore with clients the sensations they experienced. Some people have a hard time initially with slow, deep breathing. If a client says it was difficult, ask her to give it time and to practice diaphragmatic breathing for five breaths each day instead of the full ten to fifteen minutes. At the next session you can follow up and ask how her practice went. If she enjoyed the deep breathing, recommend that she practice for ten breaths twice a day. Then, check in with her again, at the next session, to see how her breathing practice went. Encourage her to work up to ten to fifteen minutes a day.

While clients are learning to breathe mindfully, you can teach them how to do the body scan, which also involves breathing mindfully. Instruct clients in both of these techniques and ask them to do the practices at different times during the day. Generally, the body scan takes about forty-five minutes, while practicing mindful breathing can take just a few moments to do. Once clients develop a daily practice of breathing mindfully for longer periods, you can encourage them to try sitting meditation.

BODY SCAN

If you already employ relaxation exercises in treating clients, the body scan might seem similar to autogenic training, progressive muscle relaxation, and other guided relaxation exercises. The body scan is similar in that the client is asked to lie or sit in a relaxed position and close or lower her eyelids and then focus on different parts of the body. The therapist then guides the client through the exercise and encourages her to practice at home as well, initially using a recorded version and then eventually on her own.

Among the differences between commonly used relaxation strategies and the body scan is that the focus is not on relaxation per se. Although most people who try the body scan report feeling relaxed during the exercise and for some time afterward, the focus of the body scan is attending to one's breathing and body using mindfulness.

In mindfulness-based stress reduction, the body scan is the first meditation technique clients are asked to commit to practicing at an intense level (Kabat-Zinn, 2005). Participants are guided through a forty-five-minute body scan and instructed to practice it six days a week for two weeks. Other mindfulness-based interventions may not include the body scan or may not ask participants to practice it as frequently or for as long.

Instructions for the Body Scan

Instructions for the body scan follow a general framework in which you invite the client to notice her breath and then allow the breath to flow into different parts of her body. As she attends with curiosity, nonjudgment, and other mindfulness qualities, encourage her to let her breath travel to the part of her body she's currently focusing on, and to imagine breathing into and out of that part of the body while attending to the process mindfully.

Begin by asking the client to lie on her back on a mat on the floor or sit in a reclining chair or a chair with footstool. If none of those options is possible, ask her to sit in the most comfortable position she can be in. Present the following instructions slowly, in a quiet and warm voice. Wherever indicated, pause for about five seconds. The exercise should take about forty-five minutes.

Therapist: You can close your eyes or lower your eyelids, or find a spot to focus on gently. Notice your breath and the movement of your belly and chest as you breathe. Just notice the breath without trying to change it in any way. *(Allow the client to breathe in and out for five breaths.)*

Now notice the toes in your left foot. Allow your breath to breathe into your toes, breathing in and out...in and out. *(Pause.)* Notice how the outsides of the toes feel. What are they touching? What sensations do you feel? Allow your breath to caress the toes. Now notice any sensations inside the toes. Breathing in and out...in and out. *(Pause.)*

Now notice the bottom of your left foot. Allow your breath to breathe into your foot, breathing in and out...in and out. *(Pause.)* Notice how the outside of the foot feels and what it is touching. What sensations do you feel? Allow your breath to caress the foot. Now notice any sensations inside the foot. Breathing in and out...in and out. *(Pause.)*

Become aware of your left leg. Allow your breath to breathe into your leg from the calf muscle to the knee, and then the thigh muscles, breathing in and out of the leg...in and out. *(Pause.)* Notice how the outside of the leg feels and what it's touching. What sensations do you feel? Allow your breath to caress the leg. Now notice any sensations inside the leg. Breathing in and out...in and out. *(Pause.)*

Now move the focus of your attention to the area of your pelvis. Notice the muscles and bones of your pelvis and allow your breath to breathe into your pelvis, breathing in and out...in and out. *(Pause.)* Notice how your skin feels and what it is touching. What sensations do you feel? Allow your breath to caress the pelvis. Now notice any sensations inside the pelvis. Breathing in and out...in and out. *(Pause.)*

Now notice the toes in your right foot. Allow your breath to breathe into your toes, breathing in and out...in and out. *(Pause.)* Notice how the outsides of the toes feel. What are they touching? What sensations do you feel? Allow your breath to caress the toes. Now notice any sensations inside the toes. Breathing in and out...in and out. *(Pause.)*

Now notice the bottom of your right foot. Allow your breath to breathe into your foot, breathing in and out...in and out. *(Pause.)* Notice how the outside of the foot feels and what it is touching. What sensations do you feel? Allow your breath to caress the foot. Now notice any sensations inside the foot. Breathing in and out...in and out. *(Pause.)*

Become aware of your right leg. Allow your breath to breathe into your leg from the calf muscle to the knee, and then the thigh muscles, breathing in and out of the leg...in and out. *(Pause.)* Notice how the outside of the leg feels and what it is touching. What sensations do you feel? Allow your breath to caress the leg. Now notice any sensations inside the leg. Breathing in and out...in and out. *(Pause.)*

Now bring your attention up toward your torso, noticing your stomach, chest, and back. Become aware of your torso and allow your breath to breathe into your torso, breathing in and out of the stomach, chest, and back...slowly in and out. *(Pause.)* Notice how the outside of your torso feels, and what it is touching. What sensations do you feel? Allow your breath to caress the torso. Now notice any sensations inside your chest and back. Breathing in and out... in and out. *(Pause.)*

Now notice the fingers of your left hand. Allow your breath to breathe into your fingers, breathing in and out...in and out. *(Pause.)* Notice how the outsides of the fingers feel. What are they touching? What sensations do you feel? Allow your breath to caress the fingers. Now notice any sensations inside the fingers. Breathing in and out...in and out. *(Pause.)*

Now notice the whole of your left arm. Allow your breath to breathe into your forearm and upper arm, breathing in and out...in and out. *(Pause.)* Notice how the outside of the arm feels. What is it touching? What sensations do you feel? Allow your breath to caress the whole arm. Now notice any sensations inside the arm. Breathing in and out...in and out. *(Pause.)*

Gently bring your attention to your shoulders. Now notice the muscles of your shoulders, allowing your breath to breathe into your shoulders, breathing in and out...in and out. *(Pause.)* Notice how the outsides of the shoulders feel. What are they touching? What sensations do you feel? Allow your breath to caress the shoulders. Now notice any sensations inside the shoulders. Breathing in and out...in and out. *(Pause.)*

Now notice the fingers of your right hand. Allow your breath to breathe into your fingers, breathing in and out...in and out. *(Pause.)* Notice how the outsides of the fingers feel. What are they touching? What sensations do you feel? Allow your breath to caress the fingers. Now notice any sensations inside the fingers. Breathing in and out...in and out. *(Pause.)*

Now notice the whole of your right arm. Allow your breath to breathe into your forearm and upper arm, breathing in and out...in and out. *(Pause.)* Notice how the outside of the arm feels. What is it touching? What sensations do you feel? Allow your breath to caress the whole arm. Now notice any sensations inside the arm. Breathing in and out...in and out. *(Pause.)*

Allow your attention to move to your neck, noticing it connected to your shoulders, holding your head upright. Bring your breath into your neck, noticing the sensations inside and outside of your neck. Breathing in and out...in and out. *(Pause.)* Let the breath warm and fill your throat. Breathing in and out...in and out. *(Pause.)*

Now move your breath upward into your head. Bring your breath into your head, noticing all the muscles in your face, the back of your head, your ears, lips, and nose. Become aware of sensations inside and outside of your head. Breathing in and out...in and out. *(Pause.)* Let the breath flow into your head. Breathing in and out...in and out. *(Pause.)* Now let the breath flow out the top of your head. Breathing into and out of the top of your head. Breathing in and out...in and out. *(Pause for ten seconds.)*

Now slowly turn your attention to your whole body, taking a few moments to attend to your body from your toes up to your head. *(Pause for two to three minutes.)* Now take a few moments to return to awareness of your environment. You can slowly open your eyes and take a moment or two to look around and move a little, while continuing to breathe and feel connected to your body moment by moment, here and now. *(Pause until your client makes eye contact or seems ready to speak or move on.)*

Review the client's experience with her. Ask her to describe areas of the body that were easy or difficult to attend to. Remind her that the goal isn't to be relaxed per se, but to attend to and become aware of and connected to her body, and to notice the temporary nature of these sensations. You can give the client an audio recording of the body scan to use between sessions. Ask her to practice the body scan daily for two weeks and then alternate the body scan with yoga starting the third week and through the fourth week.

SITTING MEDITATION

There are many forms of sitting meditation. Concentration meditation involves focusing attention on something in particular. It could be the breath or the act of breathing, an image, certain metaphors, a thought, a feeling, or a sensory experience. Another type of meditation involves just observing and noting internal and external experiences; this type of meditation is referred to as mindfulness meditation. Loving-kindness meditation is distinguished from the other types of meditation in that it's directed toward fostering the affective qualities of mindfulness: gratitude, gentleness, generosity, empathy, and loving-kindness.

For all forms of sitting meditation described below, guide clients through the meditation initially, and then have them practice at home, either on their own or while listening to a recording of the meditation instructions. Some communities may have sitting meditation groups that are open to the public; these are often offered at meditation centers. Some clients may find it helpful to meditate in a group setting, while others will find it distracting. You can discuss this option with individual clients to determine whether participating in a meditation group could help encourage their practice.

Initial Instructions for All Types of Sitting Meditation

Ask the client to sit on the floor in the lotus or half lotus position or any comfortable sitting position. The lotus position requires the person to sit on the floor cross-legged, with each foot resting on the opposite leg. In the half lotus position, the person rests only one foot on the opposite leg, with the other resting beneath. Some clients might like to sit on a *zafu* or a meditation bench. Clients who cannot sit on the floor can sit comfortably in a chair.

Whatever the sitting position, instruct the client to begin by paying attention to her posture. Have her sit with her back erect and chest open, meaning the client gently pushes her shoulder blades together and down as a way to help open the chest. The arms are relaxed, and the hands rest on the thighs or lap in an open position, with the palms facing either up or down. Have the client hold her head up, with her chin in a comfortable position.

You can tell the client that it's okay to move during the meditation, but that you encourage her to first notice the discomfort or urge to move, and then wait a few moments before moving. She may find that the discomfort or urge to move decreases as she simply observes and then turns her attention back to the meditation. In the sections that follow, I'll describe four different forms of sitting meditation: mindfulness meditation, the mountain meditation, the lake meditation, and loving-kindness meditation. In MBSR, clients are asked to gradually increase the duration of sitting meditation to forty-five minutes a day. This can consist of concentrative, mindfulness, or loving-kindness meditation; the main intention is to be still and mindful for the full forty-five minutes.

MINDFULNESS MEDITATION

Mindfulness sitting meditation involves choiceless awareness, or bare attention. *Choiceless awareness* means being aware of whatever you experience in each moment without seeking or rejecting any particular experience. Initially, you can instruct the client to continue with simple breath awareness or diaphragmatic breathing (described above) while gradually increasing her sitting time from five minutes to forty-five minutes. You can tell her to add five minutes to her sitting meditation time each week. However, it is important for the client to be accepting and patient with what she can manage and not think of it as some sort of competition.

After the client has practiced sitting meditation with a focus on mindful breathing for a week, you can encourage her to widen the stimuli she attends to in her sitting meditation practice. This might include other bodily sensations besides breathing, as well as sounds, thoughts, and feelings. Eventually, she should be able to just sit, not focusing on anything in particular—just watching whatever enters her awareness and letting it come and go while sitting quietly. Jon Kabat-Zinn describes it as "a relaxation into stillness and peace beneath the surface agitations of your mind" (2005, p. 72). Choiceless awareness can be very challenging, and initially the client may be able to do it for only a few minutes at a time. The client can intersperse choiceless awareness with concentrating on the breath or images, feelings, or thoughts.

Instructions for Mindfulness Meditation

Therapist: Now that you're seated, close your eyes or lower your eyelids. Notice your breath. Feel the air moving into your nostrils, into your body. Breathing in, and breathing out. *(Pause for ten seconds. Remember to speak slowly as you guide your client through this meditation.)*

Notice your body connected to the floor or seat. Allow yourself to feel grounded and supported by the earth, knowing as you sit here that you are connected to all things. Allowing yourself to just be right now, moment by moment.

As you breathe in and out, you'll notice that your mind begins to wander. *(Pause for ten seconds.)* Notice your thoughts, feelings, or whatever sensations come into your awareness. Observe them, letting them pass into your awareness. Then gently bring your awareness back to your breath. Breathing in, and breathing out...in and out. *(Pause for ten seconds.)*

Continue observing and not judging yourself for whatever enters your mind. Bringing your attention back to your breath, then watching it wander away again.

When you find yourself getting involved in thoughts, images, or feelings, gently and patiently bring your awareness back to your breath. Don't get upset with yourself if you have to do this frequently. With time you'll find that you move into a place that's calm and watchful and not reactive to these images and thoughts.

Continue to sit, gently bringing your awareness back to the breath whenever you find yourself dwelling in thoughts of the past or images of the future. It might help you to label these as "thought," "feeling," "image," "planning," and so on. Then return to the breath.

Breathing in and out...in and out. Continue to observe and bring your attention back to the breath whenever it wanders for the next five minutes. *(Start with five minutes and increase by five minutes or more each week, depending on the client and her goals. During the rest of the time your client is meditating, you can periodically say a word or two to help her remember to focus on the breath, such as "breathe in...breathe out" or "notice your breath.")*

Now notice your body connected to the floor or seat. Sense your hands, arms, feet, legs, shoulders, and face. When you're ready, slowly open your eyes and gently move your body. You can gently stretch out your legs and arms.

After guiding clients through mindfulness meditation, get feedback on how the experience went for them. Explore with them what seemed to go well and whether they struggled with some aspect of the meditation. If they did struggle, confirm that they will at times find it difficult to practice mindfulness meditation. Advise them that when this happens, they can practice patience with themselves. Encourage them to stick with it, maybe even adding another minute or two to their practice time.

You can also discuss how internal and external stimuli may catch their attention when meditating, and that they don't have to react or respond to these things; they can just notice or observe them. They can be nonjudging and practice letting go of their responses. As their meditation practice deepens, they might also experience various sensations as more temporary then they had previously realized.

You can also help clients generalize the skill of mindfully noticing internal and external stimuli from meditation practice to experiences throughout the day—how, even when they aren't meditating, they can begin noticing that their thoughts are just thoughts and their emotions are just emotions. Explain that meditation practice will facilitate their ability to be mindful when confronted with stressors they might encounter. You can also instruct them in informal mindfulness practices (described in chapter 5), as these practices can help them more readily respond to everyday situations with the choiceless awareness that they are developing with mindfulness meditation. Throughout the day, they can also use phrases such as "breathe in...breathe out" or "let go" as cues to deepen their moment-by-moment mindfulness.

MOUNTAIN MEDITATION

The mountain meditation is a concentrative practice in which the client focuses on the metaphor of a mountain during sitting meditation. The client attends to images of a mountain when distracting or negative thoughts or feelings enter her awareness.

Instructions for the Mountain Meditation

Therapist: Now that you're seated, close your eyes or lower your eyelids. Notice your breath. Feel the air moving into your nostrils, into your body. Breathing in, and breathing out. *(Pause for five seconds.)*

Allow yourself to imagine a mountain or large rock formation that you may have encountered in the past or seen in a picture. Notice your breathing, in and out, then imagine the solidness and unmoving nature of the mountain. Allow yourself to breathe in the solidness of the mountain, breathing in and out...in and out. *(Pause for ten seconds.)*

When thoughts, feelings, and images enter into your awareness, notice that they might be like things that can affect only the outer surface of the mountain. Breathing in solid, breathing out calm. *(Pause for ten seconds.)*

The mountain withstands changing seasons, fires, storms, and humans who build upon it or tear down things built upon it. Sometimes rocks, or even boulders, may break off. Yet all the while, the mountain itself remains solid, serene, and unmoved. Breathing in solid, breathing out calm. *(Pause for ten seconds.)*

Allow yourself to breathe in the internal sense of the mountain's solidity and balance while observing any thoughts or sensations that enter your awareness in the same way a mountain might observe a forest fire or an avalanche. Breathing in the solidity of the mountain, breathing out calm. *(Pause for ten seconds.)*

(Continue with images of the enduring solidity of the mountain for at least five more minutes. You can continue for up to twenty more minutes if your client has been practicing meditation for at least two weeks.)

Now notice your body connected to the floor or seat. Sense your hands, arms, feet, legs, shoulders, and face. When you're ready, slowly open your eyes and gently move your body. You can gently stretch out your legs and arms.

After guiding clients through this meditation, ask them to describe their experience of the meditation to you. Get feedback from clients on whether the mountain meditation was helpful or not in promoting feelings of calmness and solidity in the midst of change. Ask them what images of the mountain were most effective for them and whether any images distracted them or made it more difficult to attend mindfully to their experience. You can discuss with them how the mountain image can be a good metaphor for the interior stance of someone who practices mindfulness. Internal and external stimuli may catch their attention, but they don't have to react or respond to these things. They can maintain inner patience and acceptance as they bring their attention to images of solidness and calm. You can encourage clients to experiment with using those same images to help them feel more solid and calm when they encounter difficult situations in daily life. They can also use the phrase "solid and calm" as a cue to be mindful throughout the day.

LAKE MEDITATION

A lake is receptive and accepts whatever changes occur on the surface. Yet beneath the surface the water is still and calm. For this concentrative practice, ask the client to bring up an image of a lake that she has a connection with, either one she has visited or one she knows about.

Instructions for the Lake Meditation

Therapist: Now that you're seated, close your eyes or lower your eyelids. Notice your breath. Feel the air moving into your nostrils, into your body. Breathing in, and breathing out. *(Pause for five seconds.)*

Allow yourself to imagine a lake. What surrounds the lake? Are there soft, green banks that gently slope into the lake? Is the lake nestled between two mountain peaks? Breathing in the stillness of the lake, breathing out calm. *(Pause for ten seconds.)*

Allow yourself to be the lake and breathe with it. Explore the depths of the lake. What colors do you see? What changes in the water temperature do you experience? Breathing in the stillness of the lake, breathing out calm. *(Pause for ten seconds.)*

Notice any forms of life within the water. Fishes, turtles, otters, plants, all living in harmony. Notice any birds that may be floating on the water's surface. Breathing in the stillness of the lake, breathing out calm. *(Pause for ten seconds.)*

Look up, above the water, to observe the sky and feel the wind on the surface of the lake. Noticing the season and its coolness or warmth. Breathing in stillness, breathing out calm. *(Pause for ten seconds.)*

Now imagine a storm brewing above the lake, and experience the surface of the lake being whipped by winds and pelted with rain. Notice how the inner depths of the lake remain calm. In time the storm passes, and slowly the surface returns to stillness. Breathing in stillness, breathing out calm. *(Pause for ten seconds.)*

(Continue with images of the calm and stillness of the depths of the lake for at least five more minutes. You can continue for up to twenty more minutes if your client has been practicing meditation for at least two weeks.)

Now notice your body connected to the floor or seat. Sense your hands, arms, feet, legs, shoulders, and face. When you're ready, slowly open your eyes and gently move your body. You can gently stretch out your legs and arms.

After guiding them through this meditation, ask clients to describe what their experience of the lake mediation was like. Get feedback from them on whether the lake meditation was helpful or not in promoting feelings of stillness and calm. You can discuss how the lake image is a good metaphor for the interior stance of someone who practices mindfulness. Internal and external stimuli may catch their attention, but they don't have to react or respond to these things. They can respond with inner patience and acceptance as they bring to mind the images that help them sense the deep stillness within the lake and within themselves. As with the other meditations discussed thus far, encourage clients to bring to mind images of the lake during everyday experiences to help remind them of the deep calmness they are developing through meditation practice. They can use the phrase "still and calm" as cues to remember to be mindful.

LOVING-KINDNESS MEDITATION

Loving-kindness meditation, sometimes referred to as metta meditation, is a form of concentration meditation and is typically practiced during a sitting meditation. (*Metta* is the Pali word for "loving-kindness.") It is usually introduced to clients after they've had some experience with sitting meditation.

The general format is to guide the client through a series of images that focus on thoughts and feelings of loving-kindness. First, you have the client focus on herself. After about five minutes, ask her to focus these thoughts on someone she cares about. After another few moments, ask her to focus loving-kindness on people she doesn't know very well. Next, ask her to focus these feelings on people she doesn't like or who have been hurtful to her. The meditation then expands outward, to focus on all of creation with loving-kindness. This meditation helps develop a sense of acceptance and care, moving from oneself outward, ultimately to all systems within the universe.

Instructions for Loving-Kindness Meditation

Therapist: Now that you're seated, close your eyes or lower your eyelids. Notice your breath. Feel the air moving into your nostrils, into your body. Breathing in, and breathing out. *(Pause for five seconds.)*

Take a few moments to attend to your heart. *(Pause for five seconds.)* Feel your breath in your heart. Loving-kindness involves opening and softening the heart. If you feel comfortable doing so, you can place one or both hands over the area of your heart. Breathe into your heart...in and out...in and out. *(Pause for ten seconds.)*

Start by holding yourself in loving-kindness. As I offer some phrases for you to consider, please feel free to change them to whatever allows you to hold yourself in loving-kindness. If you find yourself distracted by other thoughts or feelings, simply return to your breath.

You might imagine yourself enfolded in the arms of someone who has loved and cared for you. Repeat these phrases to yourself as you breathe in and breathe out: May I be held in loving-kindness. May I be well in both body and mind. May I be safe from all dangers. May I be happy and free. *(Pause for ten seconds.)*

May I be held in loving-kindness. May I be well in body and mind. May I be safe from all dangers. May I be happy and free. *(Pause for ten seconds. Slowly repeat these phrases for five minutes.)*

Now turn your attention to someone you care about, maybe someone who has taken care of you or someone you love deeply. Imagine that person being held in loving-kindness. Breathing in and out. *(Pause for ten seconds.)*

May you, loved one, be held in loving-kindness. May you be well in body and mind. May you be safe from all dangers. May you be happy and free. *(Pause for ten seconds.)*

Breathing in and holding that person in loving-kindness. Breathing out and sending this beloved person loving-kindness. *(Pause for ten seconds.)*

May you be held in loving-kindness. May you be well in body and mind. May you be safe from all dangers. May you be happy and free. *(Pause for ten seconds. Slowly repeat these phrases for five minutes.)*

Now expand your heart to hold an image of a neighbor, a friend, or another more casual acquaintance you might come into contact with during the week. Hold this person in loving-kindness. *(Pause for ten seconds.)*

May you also be held in loving-kindness. May you be well in body and mind. May you be safe from all dangers. May you be happy and free. *(Pause for ten seconds. Slowly repeat these phrases for five minutes.)*

As your heart naturally opens and becomes softer with loving-kindness, you may be able to bring into your awareness with loving-kindness a person who has made life difficult for you. As you bring this person who has been difficult into your awareness, you might find your heart wanting to close. This is the natural tendency of the heart, to protect and avoid suffering.

As you stay with loving-kindness, you'll understand that a closed heart continues your suffering. Turn your attention to those who are difficult and offer an open heart.

May even you be held in loving-kindness. May even you be well in body and mind. May even you be safe from all dangers. May even you be happy and free. *(Pause for ten seconds. Slowly repeat these phrases for five minutes)*

Now allow loving-kindness to spread to all beings, all of creation, near and far. Extend loving-kindness to all beings... May all beings be held in loving-kindness. May all beings be well in body and mind. May all beings be safe from all dangers. May all beings be happy and free. *(Pause for ten seconds. Slowly repeat these phrases for five minutes.)*

Spend the next few moments with loving-kindness, bringing into awareness any being that most readily softens your heart. Bringing again the phrases to mind... May you be held in loving-kindness. May you be well in body and mind. May you be safe from all dangers. May you be happy and free. *(Pause for ten seconds.)*

Breathing in and out...in and out. Continue the phrases of loving-kindness, remembering that you can bring these images and intentions into your awareness as you go about your daily activities...remembering to hold yourself in loving-kindness throughout the day. *(Pause for ten seconds.)*

Now notice your body connected to the floor or seat. Sense your hands, arms, feet, legs, shoulders, and face. When you're ready, slowly open your eyes and gently move your body. You can gently stretch out your legs and arms.

Ask clients how the loving-kindness meditation went for them. Some clients will say that it was initially difficult for them to open their heart and extend loving-kindness to someone who hurt them. Many people experience both positive and negative emotions when first trying this meditation. With time and practice, they will experience a softening of the heart and may be able to release anger and forgive those who have hurt them.

With some clients, it may be worthwhile to suggest that they use the whole meditation time to focus on loving-kindness for themselves. You can continue to guide them through the loving-kindness meditation, keeping the focus on the client. It's difficult to truly feel love for others if you can't love yourself. So for clients who have trouble with self-esteem, self-forgiveness, depression, self-harm, or other issues that cause them to think badly of themselves, it may be effective to have them focus loving-kindness on themselves for a few practices, until they're ready to move on.

There are no studies indicating the most effective way to employ loving-kindness meditation in terms of whom to focus on. However, I think it's best to encourage including others sooner, rather than later, to help develop a better sense of the interconnectedness of all beings. Loving-kindness meditation helps clients develop the affective mindfulness qualities and can help free them from painful feelings they may have toward certain people.

WALKING MEDITATION

Walking meditation involves slowly walking as you meditate. All that's required to do this meditation is a space about five or six feet long and about two feet wide. It can be done inside or outside. Some clients may feel awkward doing this exercise, in which case they should first try it in a private place, free from distractions. If you have the space, start by conducting this exercise in the therapy room. If you take the client outside, it's best to use a quiet and private space, such as a garden or courtyard. Start by having the client do a few minutes of seated meditation with a focus on the breath.

Instructions for Walking Meditation

Therapist: Now that you're seated, close your eyes or lower your eyelids. Notice your breath. Feel the air moving into your nostrils, into your body. Breathing in, and breathing out. *(Pause for five seconds.)*

When you're ready, open your eyes, but you can keep your eyelids lowered. Slowly stand up and slowly move a few feet in one direction *(you can point out a particular place as the turnaround point),* then turn and walk back to the starting position, then turn again. *(Pause and wait for the client to stand.)*

Walk slowly, noticing each small movement you make. Breathing in and breathing out as you move.

You might bring your awareness to your toes as they push off the ground, moving your foot forward. Then notice the other foot contacting the ground on your next step. Notice the heel of the foot making contact, and then the sole of your foot contacting the surface under your foot and grounding you there. *(Pause while the client takes a few steps, then continue when she gets close to the turnaround point.)*

As you begin to turn around, notice the movement of the core of your body. Where are your hands and arms? Breathe in awareness of these parts of your body. Breathe out as you move each part.

Notice your neck and head. As you walk, slow down and become aware of some aspect of your movement in the present moment.

(For fifteen or twenty minutes, continue directing the client to move slowly and note various parts of her body and sensations she might experience as she moves. Pause often so she can focus on her movements.)

As you approach your starting place, slowly sit back down and close your eyes or lower your eyelids. Now notice your body connected to the floor or seat. Sense your hands, arms, feet, legs, shoulders, and face. When you're ready, slowly open your eyes and gently move your body. You can gently stretch out your legs and arms.

After guiding clients through this practice, spend a little time reviewing how it went for them. Some clients will note that they felt unsteady moving so slowly. You can point out that this commonly occurs when we bring conscious attention to movements that we usually aren't aware of or don't need to think about. Encourage your clients to practice at home or at work if they can find a quiet space to move in.

RESEARCH SUPPORT FOR FORMAL MINDFULNESS PRACTICES

In one study, a brief body scan meditation was found to reduce cigarette cravings and some withdrawal symptoms in smokers who had abstained from smoking overnight (Cropley, Ussher, & Charitou, 2007). This study randomly assigned participants to either a ten-minute body scan meditation or listening to a natural history passage, and then measured desire to smoke and withdrawal symptoms. In a study that compared progressive muscle relaxation to the body scan meditation (Ditto, Eclache, & Goldman, 2006), researchers found that doing the body scan produced greater parasympathetic activation than progressive muscle relaxation did. Parasympathetic activation is usually associated with feelings of relaxation. In an earlier study, researchers found that when participants engaged in the body scan prior to an experimental psychosocial stressor, they responded to the stressor with normal activation of the hypothalamic-pituitary-adrenal axis, rather than heightened activation (Greeson et al., 2001). These findings are interesting in that they indicate participants may experience greater relaxation from the body scan than traditional relaxation exercises, even though the focus of the body scan isn't relaxation. You can tell clients that they may feel more relaxed during the body scan and for some time afterward.

Two interesting studies have examined the neurological effects of loving-kindness meditation (Lutz, et al., 2008; Lutz, et al., 2009). In one study, researchers compared expert meditators to novices and measured changes in brain activation and cardiovascular functioning (Lutz et al., 2009). They found that during loving-kindness meditation, changes in the right middle insula of the brain were associated with changes in cardiovascular function, suggesting positive links between feelings of compassion and neurological and cardiovascular functioning. The changes were greater in the expert meditators compared to the novices, suggesting that long-term meditators were able to experience feelings of compassion toward others while maintaining an adaptive neurological response. In addition, during meditation both groups demonstrated changes that fostered compassion for self and others.

SUMMARY

Some type of formal meditation is usually included in mindfulness-based interventions. These types include but are not limited to the practices described above: breathing exercises, the body scan, and sitting, walking, and loving-kindness meditation. In later chapters, I'll explain how to include these formal meditation practices in interventions for specific populations and problems. The next chapter covers informal mindfulness practices.

chapter 5

Mindfulness Techniques for Informal Practice

In this chapter, you'll learn how to help clients enhance their mindfulness by incorporating mindfulness into their daily life. Informal mindfulness techniques will help your clients generalize mindfulness to all aspects of their life and deepen their understanding of mindfulness.

A variety of informal practices can help clients generalize the benefits of meditation to everyday life by encouraging them to bring mindfulness qualities to whatever they are doing during ordinary activities throughout the day. In this chapter, I'll describe and provide instructions for a variety of informal techniques: mindfulness in daily activities, observing and describing, sensory exercises, awareness of posture, yoga, and approaches that involve using poetry and inspirational writings.

Some informal mindfulness techniques involve movement or can be practiced when in motion, such as yoga and paying attention to posture. Practicing mindfulness when in motion can help clients strengthen their awareness of their body, which can provide a greater sense of being in the moment. It can also foster self-knowledge generated from important physical information that clients might ignore or not perceive if focusing on thoughts or emotions. Paying attention to the body with the intention to be mindful will increase your clients' ability to make healthy choices and respond more effectively to their environment in the present moment.

MINDFULNESS IN DAILY ACTIVITIES

Mindful attention can be brought to any aspect of life. You can instruct clients to bring moment-to-moment mindful awareness to whatever they are doing in the present. Here's an exercise that can help clients develop the intention to attend with the mindfulness qualities throughout their day.

Therapist: Before you get out of bed in the morning, take a few moments to notice your breathing. Then make the intention to attend with mindfulness throughout the day.

Let's take a few moments to discuss the mindfulness qualities of acceptance, nonjudging, nonstriving, patience, trust, openness, and letting go and what they mean to you. (*Take a few moments to talk with the client about each of these qualities and how he can recognize them throughout the day.*)

If you observe negative emotions or sensations during the course of your day, recognize them and bring the mindfulness qualities to mind. In doing so, you might notice other aspects of your experience that you weren't aware of because you were so focused on the negative emotions or sensations. For example, you might become aware of a dull pain in your lower back. As you notice that pain, bring to mind patience, acceptance, and trust. As you attend to your lower back with these intentions, you might notice the sensation in your back starting to change. You might notice your body relaxing and feelings of inner strength arising within you.

Can you think of an example of an experience in the past week in which you were focused on negative images, feelings, or sensations? (*Discuss with the client how he can bring the intention to be mindful to these negative experiences in the upcoming week.*)

This is just one example; you can explore mindfulness in many other daily activities with clients. In later chapters, you'll see that the experiences to emphasize depend on the client and his problems. By discussing and reviewing your client's daily experiences, you demonstrate to your client the importance of making an effort to think about his thinking using the mindfulness qualities.

Three-Minute Breathing Space

Informal mindfulness of breathing simply means noticing the breath throughout the day. In mindfulness-based cognitive therapy and several other approaches, this informal practice is sometimes slightly more structured (Baer, 2006) and is known as the three-minute breathing space. In this practice, clients are instructed to take one minute to consider each of three different aspects of their awareness in the present moment. Using the three-minute breathing space helps clients notice when they're becoming mindless and then refocus on the activity at hand.

Therapist: First, note the thoughts, feelings, and sensations you are experiencing right now. It is important to attend to these experiences with acceptance and non-judgment. Don't push away or avoid these experiences; just acknowledge them. (*Pause for one minute.*)

Now attend fully to your experience of breathing. Just notice breathing in and then out...in and out. (*Pause for one minute.*)

Now take a moment to move your attention to other aspects of your body and recognize and accept whatever is present to you in the moment. *(Pause for one minute.)*

Instruct clients to practice the three-minute breathing space several times each day. As they learn to use this technique to respond skillfully to daily activities, they may that find attending to even just one breath is helpful when many different demands compete for their attention. Remind clients that at any given point in time, they are free to choose their response to whatever situation they find themselves in, and that they can use the breath as a cue to respond mindfully. In this way, awareness of the breath can help reduce habitual or automatic responses to the environment.

Using Environmental Cues

Another way to become more mindful during daily activities involves using environmental cues as reminders. For example, the ringing of the telephone can serve as a reminder to tune in to the present moment (Nhat Hanh, 2000).

Therapist: You can use environmental cues to help you to remember to be mindful. For example, when the phone rings, instead of rushing to answer it, pause a moment, smile, and breathe. You can let the telephone ring a few times while you slowly walk to the phone, smiling and breathing, before you answer.

Take that time to remind yourself to be open and accepting of whoever is calling and whatever that person will say.

You can use other things in your daily routine to bring your attention to the present moment, like a knock at the door, requests from people at work, or sitting down to answer e-mail. What are some other environmental cues you can use on a daily basis to help you remember to be mindful? *(Ask the client to write these ideas down and then pick one or two to practice in the upcoming week.)*

Incorporating mindfulness into daily activities requires clients to make a conscious effort to do so each day. Discuss with clients what works and what doesn't in helping them become more mindful. Encourage them to experiment with different cues and mindful responses to those cues, such as breathing and various intentions.

Observing and Describing

Observing and describing experiences can help enhance mindfulness both during sitting meditation and as clients move through their day. While attending mindfully to inner and outer experiences, clients might find themselves reacting to strong sensations, emotions, thoughts, or images. Instead of ignoring or trying to avoid these reactions, encourage clients to take note of them by mentally pausing and just observing them. It might be helpful to think about the experience in terms of "what it is." After observing the experience and labeling it as a thought or sensation, clients can then examine it and describe what it really is.

> *Therapist:* Imagine that you're driving your car and someone cuts in front of you, nearly causing you to hit their car. You'll probably experience a surge of adrenaline and fear, and then angry thoughts and feelings may emerge. Then you might find yourself thinking about how stupid the person is, how you might have died, and so on. Then you realize that you aren't paying attention to driving and that you almost ran into someone else!
>
> To apply mindfulness, after the surge of adrenaline you would begin observing your emotions and thoughts, and then describe them to yourself. "This sensation I feel is anger. I feel threatened. Breathe...I am not hurt. My hands are tense on the steering wheel. Breathe...I can relax them and scan the cars around me now." This will help you let go of these distracting experiences so that you can bring your attention back to the task of driving, instead of being caught up in ideas and emotions that aren't pertinent to your experience in the moment. By observing and describing your experiences, you can more effectively attend to your driving—and avoid other potential accidents. You also stop yourself from responding reactively to the moment and the emotional suffering you'd experience if you were to just dwell on negative thoughts and feelings about the challenging situation that just occurred.

Encourage clients to practice observing and describing every day, especially when they're feeling strong emotions or thoughts, either positive or negative.

SENSORY EXERCISES

Sensory exercises can help develop the capacity to be mindful. Encourage clients to experiment with different sensory modalities, both when meditating and when engaging in day-to-day activities. With the exception of mindfulness-based eating exercises, research is limited on how effective these exercises are as elements of a mindfulness-based intervention. However, these exercises will help heighten clients' experience and appreciation of the present moment, and my clients have reported enjoying these types of exercises. The following examples will guide you in instructing clients on how to use their senses as the focus of informal mindfulness practice.

Smell

We humans have the ability to sense over ten thousand odors, and our sense of smell helps us respond adaptively to our environment. We can sniff out things that might be dangerous to us, such as gas or spoiled food. Certain aromas can bring us comfort, relaxation, joy, and other positive emotions, images, and memories. Sensory information about aromas is sent to the olfactory bulb in the brain, and from there it is directly processed by the limbic system, bypassing the thalamus, which is the gatekeeper for all other sensations. The limbic system plays an important role in the experience of emotions and memories. Humans have always been interested in scent and have used scent to alter our emotional and spiritual experience. You can encourage your clients to use scent to wake up to the moment. Here are some examples of how you might describe using scent to enhance mindfulness.

Therapist: "Stop and smell the roses" is a common phrase used to encourage people to slow down and appreciate the moment. You can use this as an informal practice by actually pausing and smelling something in particular or by attending to the scents in your environment in general. What are some smells that you particularly enjoy? What are some that you don't like? *(Allow the client to describe his experiences with smell.)*

To attend to your sense of smell mindfully, you might light a scented candle and bring your attention to the scent as you meditate, work, or move about the room. Or you might go outside and sit in a garden, by the water, or anywhere you like, paying particular attention to the surrounding smells. You can notice the smells entering through your nostrils, and then notice breathing them out. Experiment with different scents and notice how you might respond with different emotions and images depending on what you smell. Try not to name the smell or put words to the aromas you sense. Just notice the smell. You can practice this for as long as you like.

Sight

There is a big difference between looking and seeing. We often visually gloss over much of our environment. Informal mindfulness practice using vision encourages clients to truly see when they focus their vision on their environment. They can practice focusing their attention on seeing minute or small stimuli, such as looking closely at a flower petal. Conversely, they can practice expanding their visual attention to larger aspects; for example, observing the waves crashing along an expanse of the shoreline when walking on the beach. Here are some suggestions on how to help clients become more mindful using their sight.

Therapist: You can attend to your sense of sight in informal mindfulness practice. Using vision involves opening your eyes and attending to the colors, shapes, and designs in your environment, without trying to label what you see. So you would perceive color simply as that color, not as red, blue, or what have you. You would perceive patterns and shapes without labeling them as "book," "table," "rug," or whatever. Simply gaze at one thing or even a small aspect of something, gently accepting what you see. Alternatively, allow yourself to see a wide expanse of whatever surrounds you—the big picture. Whether you focus on the small or the grand, let judgments go and just be with what you see.

You can do this exercise inside or outside. You can also focus on a particular object, like a painting, statue, or flower arrangement. Thich Nhat Hanh, a mindfulness expert, suggests that when you truly look at something, you can see the entire universe—even in something as small as a seed. The seed exists because of the sun, the dirt, the air, the plant that bore it, and all of the molecules that make it up and existed before the seed was formed. Doing this type of visual practice as you move through your day can help you feel interconnected with all things.

Sound

We are bombarded with sounds even as we sleep. Depending on where a person lives and works, sounds can be stressful or enjoyable. Help your clients become aware of sounds they encounter on a daily basis. They can learn to use sounds to enhance their mindfulness on a day-to-day basis. Here are some examples that you can suggest for them to practice.

Therapist: You can use sound in the same way you might use your sight as a focus for paying attention in the moment. You might attend to the sounds of raindrops on the roof, for example, or the birds chirping outside as you wake up in the morning. You can focus on a particular aspect of sound or attend to all the sounds that come your way. Either way, pay attention to sounds, accepting all aspects of tone, volume, and rhythm.

For example, you can play music as you work or do other things, and occasionally pause for a moment, breathe, and attend to the rhythm, tone, or other specific aspects of the music. You can listen to other people, noting the sounds of their voices rather than the content of what they're saying. You might notice laughter, the cooing of a baby, the crying of a young child, or people shouting. Then shift to noticing the sounds of any words and what others are saying. These kinds of practices will help you experience the differences between hearing and listening.

Touch

Encouraging clients to notice how their body touches the surfaces around them as they move around in their daily activities can help ground them to wherever they are in the moment. In general, attending to sensations and experiences that heighten awareness of touch can help develop the capacity to be mindful. Some mindfulness-based interventions use touch to help couples improve their connection with each other and improve their sexual intimacy. For example, mindfulness-based relationship enhancement for couples (Carson, Carson, Gil, & Baucom, 2006) includes exercises using mindful touch. (These exercises are described in chapter 8.) Instructing couples to give light and slow massage to each other can be an exercise in touching mindfully. Here's an example of how you might introduce the informal practice of mindfulness of touch.

> *Therapist:* Notice the feel of air on your skin. Is the air still, or can you detect a breeze? Now attend to the feel of fabric against your body. What sensations do you experience? You can bring the same attention to the feeling of the surface you're sitting or standing on. Tuning in to these sensations of touch can help you bring your attention to the present moment using the mindfulness qualities. You can also notice the feel of a particular item or even a person or animal. Mindfully petting your dog or cat can help you focus on what you're sensing and experiencing in the moment.

Eating

Eating mindfully can reduce binge eating, increase clients' enjoyment of nourishing themselves, and lead to better physical health (Kristeller et al., 2006). Mindfulness-based eating interventions make use of a variety of exercises that help people develop healthy eating habits. I'll present more information on these exercises in chapter 9, in the section on interventions for eating disorders.

When prescribing eating exercises for clients, it's important to direct them to slow down and employ all of their senses with whatever they're eating. This can be done with a simple meal or snack. Initially clients may want to try it when eating alone so they aren't distracted by other peoples' eating behavior.

> *Therapist:* Mindful eating makes use of all of your senses. Let's try mindful eating of a snack. *(Offer the client something to eat, such as an orange or apple. I'll use an apple in this example.)* Take the apple into your hands and notice how it feels to the touch. *(Pause for a moment or two.)*
>
> Now take a few moments to bring it closer to your face so you can see it well. Look at it closely, noticing the different shades of color along its surface. Notice all of its surfaces, accepting and appreciating what you see. *(Pause for a moment or two.)*
>
> Now bring the apple up to your nose. What aromas do you detect? Take a few moments to breathe in the apple's scent without labeling or judging it. *(Pause for a moment or two.)*
>
> Now bring the apple to your ear. Does it make any sound? *(Pause for a moment.)*

Take your time sensing and observing the apple. Notice your body's responses in anticipation of eating it and your thoughts about the taste of the apple. Pause before you begin eating and take a few slow, easy breaths. *(Pause for a moment.)*

Once you've attended to the apple with all of your other senses, slowly take a bite and taste the food, savoring its taste and smell. Chew slowly, and attend to how your mind and body respond *(pause)*. Are you thinking ahead to the next bite, or are you thinking about something entirely different? If you're thinking about something that isn't related to the apple and your experience of it, gently return your attention to what you're doing in the moment.

As you eat, you might consider the origins of the apple you're eating. Where did it come from? Who grew the apple and harvested it? Who cleaned it and packed it? Considering all aspects of the apple, or anything you eat, can foster a greater appreciation for what you are eating. You may develop a greater sense of you interconnection with others and the planet as you consider the origins of the apple that is nourishing your body in this moment. And when you focus on the experience of eating, you can also change your relationship to food.

AWARENESS OF POSTURE

A colleague of mine who practices mindfulness often says that we forget our heads are attached to our bodies! Oftentimes people are so into their thoughts, planning, worrying, and ruminating, that they lose contact with their bodies. When this happens, people are essentially in a mindless state, as they are not attending fully to the present moment.

Becoming aware of the body throughout the day helps nurture mindfulness and brings the attention back to the present moment. Paying attention to the body can reduce health risks and foster more adaptive self-regulation. Remember the intentional systemic model of mindfulness, which says that mindfulness encourages greater awareness of the whole self and fosters healthier responses toward oneself.

Encouraging clients to bring attention to their posture in the course of daily activities can help them attend mindfully to the present moment. You can discuss with them the importance of noticing their posture as they sit down to eat, work, or relax. Bringing attention to the body can become a cue for paying attention to whatever is at hand.

Therapist: As you sit down at the table to eat, at your desk at work, or anyplace else, notice your feet planted firmly on the ground. If your feet aren't firmly on the ground, place them on the ground. Notice if you're slouching. If you are, take a breath and adjust your posture by sitting upright, with your back erect, and pulling your shoulders back a bit to open up your chest. Take a moment or two to observe your breath.

If you've been sitting for a long time, you might consider standing up and stretching, paying attention to how your body feels in that moment. If you've been moving around a lot, you might take a moment or two to be still and focus on how your body feels. Pay attention to the sensations you experience in your body. Is your body trying to tell you something? Are you feeling tense or relaxed? Are you hungry or thirsty? Do you need to do something for your health? Appreciate your body as it moves in space and time.

YOGA

Yoga is part of the intervention package used in several mindfulness-based stress reduction programs. There are many styles of yoga, but MBSR incorporates hatha yoga, which is the type most Westerners are most familiar with. Jon Kabat-Zinn, founder of MBSR, suggests that it's helpful to get on the floor every day if you can, because it helps ground you in the moment. Yoga was initially included in MBSR because it provides both another opportunity to practice mindfulness and a means to counter the muscle atrophy that patients with chronic pain and illness often experience (Kabat-Zinn, 1990).

In the fifteenth century CE, Swami Swatmarama wrote a manual on hatha yoga based on his own experiences and his understanding of previously written Sanskrit texts. Hatha yoga was developed to provide a method of purifying the body to prepare the yogi for higher meditation. The Sanskrit word *hatha* means "forceful," *ha* referring to the sun, and *tha* referring to the moon. *Yoga* means "to yoke." Thus, the term "hatha yoga" reflects the meaning of yoking the sun and moon, resulting in a powerful and balanced source of energy to ready the body for further meditation practice. It is interesting to note that the images of the sun and moon represent masculine and feminine energies, which are brought together in balance in the practice of hatha yoga.

If you aren't qualified to guide clients in yoga practice, you can still encourage them to practice at home. There are many excellent resources—books, videos, and online material—that you might recommend to clients. If you're conducting a program in a group setting and you have experience with yoga, you could guide the group through the exercises below. Alternatively, you could have someone who is certified in yoga do so. In all cases, it's important that clients consult with their physician before beginning to do yoga.

If clients want to move beyond the basic exercises below, you can recommend that they take classes with a certified yoga teacher. Classes are widely available, including at health clubs and many community centers. In addition to guiding clients through the instructions below, you can also copy these instructions and give them to clients to help them practice at home.

Yoga Instructions for Basic Poses

If you have the space and the expertise, you can introduce clients to yoga by guiding them through the eight basic beginner poses described below. In the prior session, instruct clients to wear loose clothing to the yoga session. Provide a yoga mat or ask clients to bring their own. Before beginning, have clients take off their shoes. Wherever the instructions indicate that the client is to take several slow, deep breaths or do several repetitions of a movement, be sure to pause long enough for the client to do this.

Therapist: Breathe slowly and pause between inhaling and exhaling as you go through these poses. Approach these exercises with curiosity, without judging, and without striving. As you practice these poses, don't push yourself to the point of pain. Gently challenging your body is enough to help you explore sensations, thoughts, and feelings mindfully. Stay with each pose until you feel relaxed in that position.

Begin by sitting on the floor in any position that's comfortable for you. Take a few moments to breathe deeply, taking five breaths before you move into the first pose.

Pose 1. Lie on your back with your arms alongside your body. Take five slow, deep breaths.

Stretch your arms over your head, placing them on the ground. Take five slow, deep breaths.

Bend your knees, raising them up while keeping your feet on the ground, and stretch your arms out to the side, breathing slowly and deeply.

Pose 2. Keeping your knees bent, bring them to your chest and hug your arms around them. Take five slow, deep breaths.

Staying in that position, curl your chin toward your knees, raising your head off the ground. Take five slow, deep breaths.

Bring your feet back to the floor and then straighten your legs and let them rest on the ground. Now alternate between bringing your left and right knee to your chest, breathing in as you bring you knee to your chest and then out as you release the knee and place your foot back on the ground. Do this three or four times, breathing in and out.

Pose 3. Slowly turn over and get on your hands and knees. Gently round your back, exhaling as you lift your mid-back up, tuck your pelvis down, and extend your head and neck downward. Then inhale as you gently arch your back, dropping your mid-back and raising your head and looking up. Do this slowly five times, exhaling and inhaling.

Pose 4. Staying on your hands and knees, exhale as you lift and stretch your right leg out behind you and your right arm out in front of you. Inhale and return to the all-fours position. Then exhale and extend your left leg and left arm, and inhale as you return to an all-fours position. Do this slowly five times, breathing in and out.

Pose 5. Lie back down on the floor on your back, with your arms alongside your body. Bend your knees so that your feet are positioned under your knees. Exhale and arch your back up, keeping your shoulders and arms on the ground. This pose can help release tension in your lower back. Stay in this position for three to five slow breaths.

Finish by lowering your back gently to the floor and extending your legs straight out on the floor.

Pose 6. Bend your knees again, bringing your feet back under your knees. Inhale as you lift your right leg and extend it straight up. Then exhale as you slowly bring the leg back down. Repeat this with the left leg. Do this three to five times, alternating between legs and moving and breathing slowly and evenly.

Return to the starting position, with your knees bent and feet under your knees.

Pose 7. Keeping your shoulders and upper back on the floor, gently roll your knees to the right side, allowing your left hip to come up off the ground. Turn your head to the left and stretch your left arm to the left as well. Hold this position for three to five breaths.

Return to the center position, feet on the floor beneath your knees, then gently roll your knees to the left and your head and right arm to the right. Hold this stretch for three to five breaths.

Return to the center position.

Pose 8. Extend your legs and rest your arms and hands alongside your body. Take five slow, deep breaths, noticing your body touching the ground and attending to the moment in an open and accepting way.

Return to a comfortable sitting position. Take a few minutes to sit quietly in a relaxed yet conscious position. When you're ready, slowly get up, and then enjoy your day!

Research on Yoga

In 2008, Maria Ospina and colleagues published a critical review of over four hundred clinical trials on meditation practices, including yoga. The studies reviewed included sixty-nine randomized controlled trials and thirty-six controlled clinical trials specifically evaluating yoga for a wide variety of problems. At least two reviews of yoga found positive results for reducing anxiety and depression. In general, though, they found that poor experimental design of studies on yoga makes it difficult to conclude confidently how effective yoga is for health and psychological problems.

In 2009, an excellent summary of research evaluating hatha yoga in mindfulness-based stress reduction and cognitive therapy reached similar conclusions (Salmon, Lush, Jablonski, & Sephton, 2009), stating that although initial research on the effectiveness of yoga is promising, more careful experimental studies must be conducted. The latter summary recommends that clinicians and researchers use the sequences of yoga exercises used in Jon Kabat-Zinn's original MBSR program, stating that those two yoga sequences are safe and effective poses for beginners. Salmon and colleagues also noted that the MBSR yoga sequences incorporate five important recommendations made in 1999 by T. K. V. Desikachar, a respected yoga writer and teacher:

- Starting where you are
- Ensuring that initial moves in a sequence warm up the body
- Using counterposes
- Using dynamic movements
- Interspersing counterposes between major poses

Salmon also notes that the yoga sequences used in MBSR are among the few well-defined yoga protocols, making them an excellent choice when evaluating the effectiveness of yoga from an evidence-based perspective.

POETRY AND INSPIRATIONAL WRITINGS

Haiku is an ancient form of Japanese poetry used to express an experience as succinctly as possible. Zen masters used haiku to express what is not easily expressible. Both haiku and Buddhist stories have long been used to teach Buddhism to spiritual seekers. Some mindfulness-based interventions reflect this tradition by using poetry and other inspirational writings to help clients deepen their understanding of mindfulness. Teachers of mindfulness-based approaches often share stories and poetry with clients, in both individual and group settings. And some interventions incorporate writing, reading, and sharing poetry and other inspirational writings.

A poem or inspirational phrase can be the focus of a meditation session. Encourage clients to journal their experiences and thoughts; they might even write their experiences in the form of a poem. Although some may not want to journal, even just occasionally writing about their experiences with mindfulness might be helpful. There is some evidence to suggest that journaling can improve psychotherapy outcomes in general. However, as of yet no research has looked specifically at the importance of journaling in mindfulness-based approaches, or the potential benefits of using poetry and other inspirational readings.

There's no set approach of when and how to provide readings, stories, or poems to clients. As you come across books or poetry that exemplify aspects of mindfulness you wish to emphasize, you can develop a list to give your clients. Many books are available that can help clients understand mindfulness and deepen their practice. Many are by writers from Eastern spiritual or philosophical traditions, but some are founded in Western traditions. Reading these writings with openness and curiosity can open the door to new ways of responding to mindfulness practices. Please see the resources section for a listing of some recommended poetry and other writings that you can share with your clients.

SUMMARY

In this chapter, I've reviewed many of the informal mindfulness techniques most commonly used in mindfulness-based interventions. These techniques employ a variety of methods to foster and deepen clients' mindfulness in everyday life.

Because informal mindfulness techniques can be employed in motion, they can help clients stay in touch with their bodies. This will help them become conscious of their environment and respond more appropriately. This, in turn, can help them reduce their emotional suffering and discover joy, happiness, peace, and other positive emotional states. You can use all of these mindfulness techniques with individual clients or in group settings.

The next chapter discusses methods of assessing mindfulness. These measures can provide feedback on whether clients are improving their capacity to be mindful. They can also help you evaluate the effectiveness of mindfulness-based interventions and further explore how mindfulness benefits those who practice it.

chapter 6

Measuring Mindfulness

In this chapter, I address issues in defining and assessing mindfulness for clinical research from an evidence-based perspective. I outline controversial issues and conceptual problems in defining mindfulness for the purposes of clinical assessment. I also describe issues in the development of measures of mindfulness. I give examples of innovative research on the assessment of mindfulness, suggest several mindfulness tests you can give your clients, and discuss the strengths and weaknesses of each.

The past ten years have seen development of a number of questionnaires for assessing trait and state mindfulness. Most measure trait mindfulness and have been developed since 2005. In the process of developing mindfulness measures, some scientists have reported issues related to measuring mindfulness in medical and psychological research (Baer, 2006; K. W. Brown & Ryan, 2004; Bishop et al., 2004; Grossman, 2008).

I'll discuss most of the major concerns with assessment development and design below. But first, let's consider why it's important to measure mindfulness. From a scientific standpoint, measuring mindfulness is critical in order to provide evidence that treatment outcomes are indeed the result of changes in mindfulness. If you consider mindfulness to be an independent variable, then you must be able to measure that variable to demonstrate varying degrees of mindfulness. Different degrees of mindfulness represent varying degrees of the independent variable. Measuring mindfulness before, during, and after clinical interventions allows you to understand whether mindfulness caused changes in targeted dependent variables. The dependent variables would be the specific behavioral, emotional, or cognitive symptoms that are the target of the intervention.

ASSESSING MINDFULNESS MEASURES

In order to effectively choose among the various mindfulness tests and understand their strengths and weaknesses, you need to understand some key aspects of how these measures are evaluated. In other words, it's important to be able to assess the effectiveness of the assessments. Three key concepts in this regard are normative samples, reliability, and validity.

Normative Samples for Mindfulness Measures

The *normative sample* for a test is just what it sounds like: the norms for that test. The normative sample is important because it allows you to compare clients' test scores to the average score of the normative sample and determine how much their scores deviate from the mean. Establishing a normal curve for the tests scores provides a method for determining how mindful clients are compared to the norm. Without norms, it's impossible to make sense of any given score.

Interpretation of test scores should always be made in light of the characteristics of the people making up the normative sample. Normative samples that reflect the general population in terms of important demographics, such as age, education, race, and gender, allow for greater generalizability of the test. Unfortunately, most of the available mindfulness tests have used relatively restricted normative samples, and often the normative sample is based on college students, local participants, or small numbers of participants.

When choosing a mindfulness test, it's critical to choose one that has a normative sample that includes data on people who are similar to the population you're working with. If such norms aren't available, you might have to create your own local norms in order to make sense of your clients' responses to a mindfulness measure. To do so, keep a record of client scores on any measure of mindfulness that you employ. Once you get about ten scores for a given measure, you can calculate the average of your clients' scores. This will indicate the average level of mindfulness for the type of clients you work with. You can then compare an individual client's scores to the mean to determine if your client's score is below, average, or above average compared to other clients you work with.

More work is needed to improve the normative samples of all the mindfulness measures currently available.

Determining Reliability

In the field of assessment, "reliability" indicates how consistent individual scores will be across time, with different scorers, and within the test items. Test reliability allows you to determine whether changes in test scores reflect true changes in the concept measured or are due to error. While there is always some fluctuation in most biopsychosocial responses, test reliability helps you determine how much change needs to occur in your client's response before you can consider it a "true" difference. Good reliability is a prerequisite for evaluating tests for validity. In other words, if a test isn't reliable, then whatever it is intended to measure isn't being measured consistently, indicating that the test may measure different things at different times.

Test-retest reliability reflects the consistency of scores over time when the same person takes the same test later under similar conditions. However, if a person does something to change the characteristics measured by the assessment, such as participating in an effective intervention, the scores should change. If the test has high test-retest reliability, this indicates there really was a change in the characteristic, rather than the change in score being due to low test-retest reliability.

Inter-scorer reliability indicates how consistent the score will be regardless of who scores the tests. *Inter-item reliability* indicates the consistency of the rating of individual test items within a test. On a test with high inter-item reliability, the individual test items tend to be measuring a similar concept or characteristic.

Generally, a correlation coefficient is used to analyze these different types of reliability. Test-retest reliability is derived by comparing the relationship between scores on the same test taken multiple times by the same group of people. Inter-scorer reliability is calculated by comparing scores derived by different scorers for the same test. Inter-item reliability is determined by correlations between individual items and subtest scales or total scores for the entire test.

In general, the more objective the test is and the easier it is to score correctly, the more likely it will be reliable. Here, "objective" means the tests items to be scored are specific and address observable behavior. Tests that are easy to score have items that can be clearly judged and evaluated and scoring directions that are specific. An example of the differences between objective and subjective test items would be a multiple-choice item versus a brief essay item. A multiple-choice item provides specific responses for the test taker to choose from, making scoring straightforward. A brief essay item, on the other hand, is open-ended, and raters may judge answers differently depending on their expectation of what a good answer is. Essay tests can be made more objective if raters are provided with specific criteria for assessing the answer. However, even judging whether answers meet various criteria involves some degree of subjective evaluation, thereby reducing the objectivity of the rater.

The best way to get useful results is to employ measures of mindfulness that have high inter-scorer reliability, high inter-item reliability, and high to moderate levels of test-retest reliability. If a test doesn't have high inter-scorer reliability, results may vary according to scorer, and therefore it won't be a trustworthy measure. High inter-item reliability indicates that test items are measuring similar aspects of the same construct. Measures of trait mindfulness should have high levels of test-retest reliability because a trait or disposition shouldn't change much over time. You could use trait measures to compare novice to experienced practitioners of mindfulness. Alternatively, they could be used to assess changes in mindfulness after an eight-week mindfulness-based intervention. On the other hand, measures of state mindfulness, which are designed to be sensitive to changes in state mindfulness, will have lower test-retest reliability, as state changes might occur over a short period of time. So you could give a measure of state mindfulness before and after a sitting meditation exercise to assess whether the client experienced greater state mindfulness after meditating. With measures that have subscales, individual items should correlate more highly with the scale they are assigned to than the other subscales. All items should correlate with the total score of the test. I will discuss the reliability of several commonly used mindfulness measures later in this chapter.

Measuring Validity

In regard to assessment, "validity" indicates how well a test measures what it's intended to measure. Many factors influence the validity of a test, including normative samples, reliability, the operational definition used to define what the test is measuring, and the creation and selection of items. I've already discussed issues in regard to norms and reliability. Additional important aspects of validity to consider are the test's face validity and construct validity, including content-related and empirical criterion-prediction approaches.

FACE VALIDITY

Face validity refers to whether a test appears to respondents to be measuring what it's supposed to measure. Test constructors believe that some level of face validity is important for increasing motivation to take the test. In other words, clients are less likely to attend to a test and take it seriously if it doesn't seem relevant to them. On the other hand, very high face validity can lead to *response bias*, including *social desirability bias*—the unconscious desire to be accepted by and pleasing to others or to be seen as acceptable in light of what most people in a culture think is socially acceptable. In other words, if it's clear what the test is trying to assess, it's easier for subjects to adjust or fake their answers.

Test developers can reduce some of the negative effects of face validity in several ways: by including validity scales that assess for response bias, by reverse scoring some items, and by including neutral items that might confuse the test taker about the true nature of the test. *Validity scales* consist of items that are included in a test to determine if respondents might be exaggerating their responses, answering inconsistently, not answering truthfully, and/or responding in a defensive manner to the test items. High scores on the validity scales indicate the results of the test for a particular individual is probably invalid and not usable. None of the mindfulness measures currently available includes validity scales. However, some do use reverse-scored items or word test items in the negative. For example, MAAS items are all phrased in the negative to reduce face validity.

CONSTRUCT VALIDITY

Construct validity refers to how well the test measures what it's supposed to measure. There are several ways to provide support for a test's construct validity, and the more types of support test developers can provide, the stronger the test's construct validity. Construct validity takes time to establish and can involve various sources of information. Examples of approaches that can provide evidence for the construct validity of mindfulness measures are developmental changes, correlations with other tests, factor analysis, internal consistency, convergent and divergent validation, and results of experimental interventions.

Content-related and criterion-prediction validity are two types of validity that are often used to provide evidence of construct validity for mindfulness measures. *Content-related validity* comes from creating items based on expert opinions as to characteristic responses in relation to a particular trait or concept to be measured. In the case of most mindfulness measures, researchers create items that they think tap into responses that reflect mindfulness. Test constructors might interview experts in mindfulness and meditation and solicit information and suggestions for potential test items. Others might derive test items from the operational definition of mindfulness that they are studying and may not get feedback from people who actually practice mindfulness. Once they've created a list of items, test constructors usually test the items with a pilot group. Then, based on the responses, they delete items or add new ones. Then the test is given to a larger group of people. Depending on the results with this larger group, the test may be further refined.

Many mindfulness measures are tested on groups of college students, nonclinical samples, and mindfulness meditators with varying degrees of experience. Group scores are analyzed using factor analysis to determine the strength of the factor structure of a test. *Factor analysis* is a method used to evaluate whether items on a test truly correspond to the traits the test is intended to measure. For example, the Toronto Mindfulness Scale purports to measure two aspects of mindfulness: decentering and curiosity. A factor analysis of the test items should provide some support that the test actually measures these two components of mindfulness.

Convergent and *divergent validation* approaches to construct validity compare a given assessment with tests that measure similar aspects of mindfulness and tests that should not be correlated with mindfulness. Tests that measure similar qualities of mindfulness should provide convergent validity, and those that assess qualities not correlated with mindfulness should provide divergent validity.

The biggest problem with using a content-related approach to determine construct validity is that it is difficult to prevent response biases such as social desirability bias, exaggeration, lying, or lack of awareness. None of the mindfulness measures currently available effectively controls for response bias. In some of the studies these measures have been based on, participants are asked to complete a measure of social desirability bias, like the Marlow-Crowne Social Desirability Scale, along with the mindfulness measure. If respondents score high on the measure of social desirability bias, their mindfulness score might not be valid.

Criterion-prediction validity is established by demonstrating how well a measure predicts performance in a variety of activities, including other tests. *Concurrent prediction* compares scores on the new test with scores, ratings, or performance on some other test or activity that should be related to the construct being measured. For example, skill in attending to a specific task should be related to mindfulness, with higher scores on attention related to higher mindfulness scores. Another example would be correlating scores between a mindfulness measure and a personality test measuring agreeableness and conscientiousness.

Predictive validity can help determine how well a mindfulness measure will predict something over time. For example, scores on a mindfulness measure might predict the extent of participants' stress response to a painful medical intervention in the future. Another example is assessing whether mindfulness scores predict improvement in symptoms of depression after completing a mindfulness-based intervention for depression. Both of these are examples of using experimental interventions to provide support for predictive validity.

Test developers also examine the internal consistency of a test's items to find support for construct validity. *Internal consistency* means scores on different test items are correlated with the total score of the test itself. Most of the mindfulness measures currently available provide acceptable internal consistency correlation coefficients. Another way to assess internal consistency is to compare responses on individual items for high scorers versus low scorers. If an item fails to distinguish between the two groups, the item is revised or taken out of the test. Internal consistency provides only limited support for construct validity, as it really only provides data on how well the items within a test relate to each other, not on how well the test actually measures what it purports to assess.

Another approach for evaluating construct validity is to determine what, if any, developmental changes are associated with the capacity to be mindful. For example, should the capacity to be mindful increase with age as the brain matures and the person has more opportunities to practice mindfulness? Determining developmental changes in mindfulness can be tested by comparing mindfulness scores between different age groups.

CONCEPTUAL AND PSYCHOMETRIC ISSUES IN MEASURING MINDFULNESS

If you are to select the most fitting assessment of a particular client or problem, you need to understand the distinctions between different measures and the concepts underlying them. For example, the underlying definition of mindfulness may differ from one test to the next, or tests may measure different mindfulness qualities. You'll also need to be aware of potential pitfalls, such as the limits of self-reporting and issues with how the reliability and validity of various tests were established. Another concern with using mindfulness measures is being able to interpret the score. Does a client's score indicate low, average, or high levels of mindfulness? Some tests can give you good information regarding individual scores, while others can't.

Differences in Definitions of Mindfulness

In designing measures of mindfulness, difficulties arise at the outset because of the varying definitions of mindfulness. As described in chapter 1, there are different opinions about what mindfulness is, even among experts on mindfulness. An example of this is the different operational definitions offered by two groups of mindfulness researchers. Developers of the Toronto Mindfulness Scale define mindfulness as a temporary frame of mind, or *state,* of "(a) the intentional self-regulation of attention to facilitate greater awareness of bodily sensations, thoughts, and emotions; and (b) a specific quality of attention characterized by endeavoring to connect with each object in one's awareness (e.g., each bodily sensation, thought, or emotion) with curiosity, acceptance, and openness to experience" (Lau et al., 2006, p. 1447). Developers of the Mindfulness Awareness Attention

Scale, on the other hand, define mindfulness as a disposition, or *trait*, of having "enhanced attention to and awareness of current experience or present reality" (K. W. Brown & Ryan, 2003, p. 822). There are a couple of differences to highlight in these operational definitions of mindfulness. The TMS assesses mindfulness as a state. In contrast, the MAAS assesses mindfulness as a trait. A second difference between the definitions underlying the two tests is that the TMS assesses not only attention, but also some of the mindfulness qualities, specifically curiosity, acceptance, and openness, whereas the MAAS only measures attention. It is important to consider these distinctions because they mean the tests are measuring different aspects of mindfulness. Therefore, it's a good idea to notice what is being measured when choosing an assessment device for a particular clinical purpose. (I'll explore this issue in greater detail later in the chapter.)

Measuring Different Dimensions of Mindfulness

Mindfulness could be considered a multifaceted concept, and some of the available measures assess different dimensions of mindfulness with specific populations in mind such as college students, long-term meditators, or clients with borderline personality disorder. Ruth Baer and colleagues (Baer, Walsh, & Lykins, 2009) designed the Five Facet Mindfulness Questionnaire to assess different dimensions of mindfulness that were formerly measured by separate assessments. Considering different dimensions of mindfulness and how they can be independently assessed could lead to a more comprehensive and acceptable assessment of mindfulness. Whether the FFMQ is capable of providing such an assessment remains to be seen, as the FFMQ is quite new and research on it is limited.

It is important to know which dimensions of mindfulness are being measured by various assessments. Knowing what a measure can validly evaluate allows you to analyze research that you use to support your clinical work. For example, it is important to note that the MAAS assesses only awareness of and attention to the current moment and not many of the other aspects of mindfulness, such as acceptance, nonjudging, and openness, which are important qualities that have been shown to improve with mindfulness practice.

Researchers' Limited Understanding of Mindfulness

Another concern is that some researchers who are developing new measures of mindfulness may be limited in their knowledge of Buddhist thinking and lack experience with Buddhist meditation (Grossman, 2008), the foundation of modern mindfulness practices. The measures these researchers create may not be using traditional Buddhist concepts of mindfulness and might be assessing something other than mindfulness from a Buddhist perspective. Before you give a mindfulness measure, review the items to determine whether the test is getting at the concepts of mindfulness that you think are important for your client.

Problems with Clients' Understanding of Test Items

There may be significant differences in how clients understand the scaled items of a test (Grossman, 2008). Responses may be influenced by the client's understanding of her own personal mindfulness practice. For clients who have no understanding of mindfulness practice, responses might be based on experiences unrelated to mindfulness. Grossman (2008) gives the example of how a college student with limited experience with mindfulness or meditation might respond very differently than a long-term practitioner of mindfulness meditation on one item of the Kentucky Inventory of Mindfulness Skills (Baer, Smith, & Allen, 2004): "I notice how foods and drinks affect my thoughts, bodily sensations and emotions." The act of noticing may be different for a college student versus a long-term meditator. The college student might notice that a night of eating and drinking poorly at a party makes her feel bad the next morning, while a long-term meditator might notice the moment-to-moment differences in how she responds to different types of food and drink that she consumes.

The Limits of Self-Reporting

All of the mindfulness scales currently available rely on self-report and don't have validity scales (items designed to indicate how truthful and accurate the subject's responses are). There might be potentially significant differences between how mindful a person is and that person's self-report of mindfulness. Other problems that must be considered when interpreting the results of these tests include social desirability bias, honesty in responses, and awareness of one's capacity to be mindful. These problems are common with all self-report measures. However, studies have found that responses to several of the mindfulness measures were not significantly influenced by social desirability bias (Lau et al., 2006; K. W. Brown & Ryan, 2003).

Issues with Measuring Validity

Another concern to consider when choosing mindfulness measures is that some were developed based on studies of long-term practitioners of mindfulness. Other mindfulness measures were created using responses from college students and other participants who had little or no experience with mindfulness. There may be biases in these tests based on the populations used to develop them.

In validating assessment instruments, an important step for test developers is to find similar measures of the construct they are measuring and correlate performance on those measures with scores obtained from the measure they're developing. This is known as *concurrent validity*. But when developing tests of constructs that haven't been assessed before, there are no tests available to compare them to. Because all of the measures of mindfulness are new, there is no "gold standard" mindfulness test that can be used to validate them. Instead, developers have had to use tests of other constructs similar to mindfulness to demonstrate concurrent validity. For example, scores on personality measures of "agreeableness" and "openness to new experiences" have been shown to be positively correlated with some measures of mindfulness. Test designers have also used tests of constructs that aren't compatible with mindfulness to demonstrate divergent validity. For example, a measure of neuroticism should be negatively correlated with a measure of mindfulness.

Some researchers are concerned that there is confusion between mindfulness itself and the outcomes of mindfulness or the skills related to mindfulness (K. W. Brown et al., 2007a). Examining the measures of mindfulness currently available makes it clear some test developers include such concepts as decentering and acceptance in their concept of mindfulness. The question remains: Are these concepts part of mindfulness, or a side product of mindfulness?

NEW AVENUES FOR EXPLORATION

One approach to validating measures of mindfulness might be to assess behavioral, emotional, physiological, or social factors related to mindfulness. An example might be to measure anxiety levels, heart rate, respiration, and performance on a stressful task and then compare these factors for research participants who score high on a mindfulness measure versus those who score low on the measure. Researchers are beginning to look into using this type of approach to provide construct validity for the mindfulness tests they develop.

It would be good if measures of mindfulness not based solely on self-report were available. Some researchers suggest developing qualitative assessment approaches. These approaches might use interview data that includes not only what clients report about their emotional and cognitive responses, but also observation of behaviors.

Other researchers suggest that it would be helpful for studies to focus on assessing mindfulness via the supposed consequences or outcomes of mindfulness. Examples might be assessing whether mindfulness interventions lead to improvement in well-being or whether loved ones report changes in participants' behavior as a result of mindfulness training. As discussed in chapter 1, examining the biopsychosocial benefits of mindfulness practice might help us understand the underlying mechanisms of changes that occur due to developing mindfulness.

APPROACHES TO MEASURING MINDFULNESS

Now that you have a better idea of the conceptual problems and psychometric issues in the development of mindfulness measures, you're in a better position to evaluate the results of mindfulness measures that you use with your clients. Before turning to discussion of specific tests, I'll briefly discuss general approaches to measuring mindfulness. Mindfulness is a multifaceted concept and can be measured using a variety of approaches. You might choose different approaches and types of measures depending on what aspects of mindfulness you're interested in and the purpose of the assessment. Among the many potential approaches are self-report, social validation, observation or performance, and physiological response. You might choose just one approach or combine several to achieve a more comprehensive and multifaceted assessment of the client's mindfulness.

Self-Report

Self-report mindfulness measures are the most commonly used method for assessing mindfulness. For the most part, these measures are quick to give and cost-efficient, most of them taking only minutes to complete and score. You can use a state measure of mindfulness to assess current levels of mindfulness, giving it right after a client participates in a mindfulness exercise. (Because of the way the TMS is written, it's best to give it only after a mindfulness practice, not before and after.) Alternatively, you can select from several trait measures of mindfulness depending on what aspects of mindfulness you're interested in assessing. These trait measures of mindfulness can be administered before clients participate in a mindfulness-based intervention, halfway through the intervention, and again after the intervention.

Most mindfulness measures can be given to older children, adolescents, and adults. For example, the Mindfulness Attention Awareness Scale has a fifth-grade reading level. The adolescent version of the MAAS, the Mindful Thinking and Action Scale for Adolescents (MTASA), can be given to children with a third- or fourth-grade reading level (West & Loverich, 2009).

The main concern with these measures of mindfulness is that they're new and have only limited research support. Most have adequate reliability in terms of inter-item consistency. Most have limited empirical support for construct validity. However, more research is being reported that generally supports the content, concurrent prediction, and predictive validity of these measures (Baer et al., 2009). Factor analysis studies tend to support the structure of the total scale scores and, for some tests, subscale scores as well (Baer, 2006).

Social Validation

Social validation refers to assessing client behavior by asking significant others, including clinicians, to rate current behavior or changes in behavior to determine whether an intervention is effective. This might involve asking the client's spouse, parents, friends, or teachers to rate various aspects of the client's outward expression of mindfulness or making such ratings yourself. You might ask significant others to independently record how often and for how long a client practices a mindfulness technique or particular behaviors associated with mindfulness. For example, ratings of skill in attending to particular events might be related to mindfulness. These types of ratings are typically used for children and other populations who might have difficulty rating themselves.

Observation or Performance

You might be interested in how changes in the capacity to be mindful affect problematic behavior, cognitions, and emotional responses. You can create tasks for your clients to engage in to determine whether they improve their responses in a variety of situations. For example, you can ask clients to role-play responses to several stressful scenarios and rate their facility at responding to the role play before and after participating in a mindfulness-based stress reduction intervention. Another example would be administering the Conners' Continuous Performance Test II, a computerized test of visual attention and vigilance, before and after a mindfulness-based intervention for attention deficit disorder (Conners & MHS Staff, 2000).

Currently there are no standard observation- or performance-based protocols for assessing mindfulness. It may be that this approach calls for more individualized measures based on the symptoms addressed in a mindfulness-based intervention or particular aspects of mindfulness related to behavioral responses. To improve the validity of performance-based approaches, it's important to use assessment tools that have been shown to have acceptable norms, reliability, and validity.

Physiological Response

There are many different types of physiological markers that can be used to assess biological changes related to changes in psychosocial functioning. The more commonly used physiological measures assess changes in the central nervous system, autonomic nervous system, and immune system. In general, it's believed that as people increase their capacity to be mindful, changes in their physiological makeup should occur. These changes might include enhancement of immune system functioning; changes in the autonomic system that involve greater parasympathetic response to stress, rather than the flight-or-fight response of the sympathetic nervous system; and increases in the complexity and number of connections within the brain and central nervous system.

Evaluating the central nervous system involves measuring changes in brain function and structure. These changes can be measured using a variety of techniques, including electrical electroencephalography (EEG), magnetic resonance imaging (MRI), and neurochemical tests. Most of these types of measures are expensive and time-consuming, cannot be administered in group settings, and require significant expertise. Some of these methods are invasive; for example, neurochemical analysis requires going beyond the skin to take blood samples.

EEG is one of the least expensive and least invasive measures of central nervous system functioning, but it does require time and considerable expertise. Some clinicians are trained in EEG assessment and are able to include it in their clinical activities. If EEG assessment is available, it might be informative to measure certain aspects of functioning related to consciousness and alert attention for some types of clients being trained in mindfulness. For example, when a mindfulness-based approach is used to treat attention deficit/hyperactivity disorder, an EEG assessment may be helpful in determining whether changes in EEG responses were associated with focused attention and thus related to changes in mindfulness.

Autonomic nervous system functioning can be measured more efficiently and less expensively than central nervous system functioning. You can assess heart rate, skin temperature, muscle tension, blood pressure, and respiration rate as indicators of autonomic nervous system functioning. This type of assessment can be elaborate or simple, depending on the accuracy required for a particular problem to be assessed. An example of a simple measure is to assess heart rate by taking the client's pulse. Inexpensive monitors can be used to measure heart rate. For more accurate and detailed assessments, you can purchase physiological assessment systems that measure heart rate, respiration rate, muscle tension, blood pressure, and so on. Most of these systems require some training; however, several professional organizations, as well as the makers of the assessment systems, offer the needed training programs. The Association of Applied Psychophysiology and Biofeedback (APPB) and the Biofeedback Certification Institute of America (BCIA) are two good sources for information on recommended equipment and training. Because autonomic nervous system functioning is easily measured, it is a good method to use to assess changes in physiological functioning that occur with mindfulness training.

Summing Up Measuring Mindfulness

In this section, I have reviewed approaches to measuring mindfulness. I have also discussed important conceptual issues and psychometric problems you should consider when choosing the best measure of mindfulness for your purposes in wanting to assess mindfulness. Self-report measures of mindfulness and assessing changes in autonomic nervous system functioning might be the most time- and cost-efficient and useful assessment methods available to you. These can be easily incorporated into your clinical practice. Data from these measures can be used to determine whether your clients are benefiting from practicing mindfulness and meditation. In the next section, I discuss three currently used self-report measures of mindfulness.

MINDFULNESS TESTS

Over the past few years, several tests of mindfulness have been reported in the research literature. I've chosen to focus on three of these tests, as they are the most frequently used and have more research support than the other tests: the Mindful Attention Awareness Scale (MAAS), the Five-Facet Mindfulness Questionnaire (FFMQ), and the Toronto Mindfulness Scale (TMS).

Mindful Attention Awareness Scale

Kirk Brown and Richard Ryan first reported on the MAAS in 2003. To date, the MAAS is the mostly widely used mindfulness scale. The MAAS has fifteen items phrased to reflect the absence, not presence, of mindfulness. The researchers used this approach to help reduce social desirability bias. Respondents are asked to rate how often they have experiences of being on automatic pilot, preoccupied, and not paying attention to the present moment. Each item is rated on a 6-point Likert-type scale, from almost always to almost never.

Brown and Ryan (2003) consider the MAAS to be a trait measure of a person's general tendency to be attentive to and aware of present-moment experience in daily life. The test has a single factor structure and provides one total score.

The MAAS is based on a definition of mindfulness as enhanced attention to and awareness of current experience or present reality. The MAAS was developed to be valid within the general population regardless of meditation experience. The test was created using college students as well as general adult samples. Test-retest reliability was evaluated with sixty college students over a four-week period, resulting in intraclass correlation of 0.81, which was considered to be acceptable.

The test developers provide support for convergent and divergent validity of the MAAS as it is correlated in expected directions with a variety of measures, including tests of personality traits and emotional and physical well-being. They also compared scores of experienced meditation practitioners to a matched sample of a general adult community and found that experienced meditators scored significantly higher on the MAAS than people who don't meditate. They also found positive correlations between MAAS scores and the number of years meditating and whether practitioners felt their practice influenced their daily life. In another study, researchers gave the MAAS before and after patients with cancer participated in a mindfulness-based stress reduction intervention (Carlson & Brown, 2005). Results indicated that higher MAAS scores, both before and after the intervention, were related to less negative emotions and lower stress. Interestingly, the researchers didn't assess whether increases in mindfulness occurred as a result of the intervention, perhaps because it wasn't a randomized trial.

In a recently reported randomized trial, MAAS scores significantly improved for participants of MBSR treatment compared to the control group at the end of treatment (Shapiro, Brown, & Bittlingmayer, 2009). The researchers also found that higher pretreatment scores on the MAAS were associated with higher post-treatment MAAS scores, as well as greater subjective well-being, empathy, and hope, and less perceived stress and rumination at two and twelve months after participating in the program.

The Mindful Thinking and Action Scale for Adolescents was recently reported by Angela West and Tamara Loverich (2009) as a downward extension for adolescents. It has a third-grade reading level. However, the MAAS was found to be a more valid measure of mindfulness for young people with at least a fifth-grade reading level.

Five Facet Mindfulness Questionnaire

Ruth Baer, Gregory Smith, Jaclyn Hopkins, Jennifer Krietemeyer, and Leslie Toney published the Five Facet Mindfulness Questionnaire in 2006. This measure has thirty-nine items, each rated on a 5-point Likert-type scale, from never or very rarely true to very often or always true. They developed the FFMQ in order to incorporate dimensions of mindfulness measured by five of the trait measures of mindfulness already in use.

The test developers conceptualized mindfulness as a construct with multiple facets and proposed that different mindfulness measures might be measuring different facets of mindfulness. In order to create a test that assesses these facets of mindfulness, they combined and correlated items from the Cognitive and Affective Mindfulness Scale (Feldman, Hayes, Kumar, Greeson, & Laurenceau, 2007), the Freiburg Mindfulness Inventory (Bucheld, Grossman, & Walach, 2001; Walach, Buchheld, Buttenmüller, Kleinknecht, & Schmidt, 2006), the Kentucky Inventory of Mindfulness Skills (Baer et al., 2004), the Mindful Attention Awareness Scale (K. W. Brown & Ryan, 2003), and the Southampton Mindfulness Questionnaire (Chadwick et al., 2008).

The FFMQ was developed using over six hundred undergraduate students, so it needs to be normed with other populations, including clinical samples and people with experience in mindfulness meditation. No data was reported on test-retest reliability.

Construct validity of the FFMQ was evaluated by statistical analyses of the combined mindfulness measures, resulting in support for the multifaceted construct of mindfulness. Item analysis and factor analysis resulted in five subscales that were supported by confirmatory factor analysis: describing, observing, acting with awareness, nonjudging of inner experience, and nonreactivity to inner experience. Internal consistency scores were acceptable and ranged from 0.71 to 0.91. FFMQ scores are reported to be higher for experienced meditators compared to nonmeditating individuals, to correlate with measures of psychological adjustment, and to improve after participating in a mindfulness meditation program (Baer et al., 2009).

Toronto Mindfulness Scale

Mark Lau, Scott Bishop, Zindel Segal, and colleagues reported on the first state measure of mindfulness in 2006. The Toronto Mindfulness Scale has thirteen items that assesses the capacity of respondent to evoke mindfulness within a brief period of time. Each item is rated on a 5-point Likert-type scale, from not at all to very much.

Lau and colleagues define mindfulness in terms of two aspects—curiosity and decentering—and designed the TMS to assess these two aspects. *Decentering* refers to an intentional self-regulatory state in which a person observes thoughts, feelings, and sensations with greater awareness. Curiosity refers to how mindfulness requires people to pay attention with curiosity, acceptance, and openness to each "object" of their experience.

The test developers used expert opinion from highly experienced mindfulness meditation instructors to create the test items. Population samples used to evaluate the TMS comprised almost four hundred participants and people with and without meditation experience. Test-retest reliability was not reported.

Construct validity research suggests support for the two factors of curiosity and decentering. The test developers provide support for convergent and divergent validity of the TMS, as it correlated in expected directions with a variety of measures, including assessments of personality traits, emotional well-being, and cognitive functioning. Experience with mindfulness meditation correlated positively with TMS scores. Internal consistency scores were good: 0.95. TMS scores improved in a group participating in a mindfulness-based stress reduction program. Lau and colleagues also found that decentering scores significantly predicted intervention outcomes.

ASSESSMENT RECOMMENDATIONS

All three of the mindfulness measures reviewed above have adequate to good construct validity as indicated by research reported on each measure. These measures also have good face validity and are easy to administer and score. However, a significant problem with these measures is that there is no information available on test-retest reliability except for one report on the MAAS. Kirk Brown and Richard Ryan (2003) found that the MAAS had acceptable test-retest reliability. Not having information on test-retest reliability is a concern; without this information, it remains unclear whether these tests are consistently measuring mindfulness. Hopefully researchers will soon begin reporting on this important aspect of mindfulness measures.

A second noteworthy problem is that none of the measures used normative samples that were representative of the general population. This makes it difficult to interpret client scores on these measures, as there is no way to know for sure whether clients are reporting levels of mindfulness that are significantly different from those of the average person. Until normative samples are determined and published, you might have to create your own local norms to help you interpret client scores.

The MAAS, FFMQ, and TMS all appear at the end of this chapter. These assessments are included only for your information. If you'd like to use them in your practice, you'll need to obtain permission to do so. To help you decide which you might want consider using with your clients, I'll briefly mention the overall strengths and weaknesses of each.

Mindful Attention Awareness Scale

The Mindful Attention Awareness Scale is currently the most used measure of trait mindfulness. The most significant weakness of the MAAS is that it measures only one aspect of mindfulness: current attention and awareness. It doesn't assess other, very important facets, including acceptance, nonjudgment, and openness, and all of the other cognitive and affective qualities of mindfulness. However, the MAAS has adequate to good test-retest reliability, internal consistency, and convergent and divergent validity. MAAS scores tend to correlate well with other measures of mindfulness. You can give the MAAS to clients who have at least a fifth-grade reading level.

Five Facet Mindfulness Questionnaire

The Five Facet Mindfulness Questionnaire is currently the most comprehensive measure of mindfulness available, as it measures five dimensions of mindfulness. It has adequate to good internal consistency and construct validity. Limitations of the FFMQ are that it has been normed only with undergraduate college students and that there is no data on its test-retest reliability. You might have to establish local norms with your clinical population if you use the FFMQ. The FFMQ requires more time to take, as it is longer than all the other mindfulness measures. If you need a quick assessment of mindfulness, you might want to use the MAAS, which has thirteen items, instead of the FFMQ, which has thirty-nine. If you want to give a client a more comprehensive measure of mindfulness, you would give the FFMQ.

Toronto Mindfulness Scale

If you're interested in assessing state mindfulness, currently the only state mindfulness test available is the Toronto Mindfulness Scale. It's quick to give and easy to score. The TMS can be given to clients right after a mindfulness-based exercise to determine their current state of mindfulness. You can track these scores over time to determine whether clients are experiencing a deepening of mindfulness as they progress through the mindfulness-based program. You could also ask clients to fill out the TMS after practicing exercises on their own, between sessions. These scores can help you determine whether clients are experiencing difficulty practicing in their day-to-day environment or becoming independent in practicing mindfulness.

SUMMARY

In this chapter, I described methodologies used to develop measures of mindfulness, as well as methods of assessing the reliability and validity of these measures. I also discussed some of the problems and difficulties in developing measures of mindfulness. I described the three most frequently used measures (the MAAS, FFMQ, and TMS), along with their strengths, weaknesses, and recommended uses. These three measures appear below. Using these measures will help you assess whether your clients really do become more mindful after participating in mindfulness-based interventions.

The next chapter provides a road map to help you develop mindfulness-based treatment protocols that are evidence based. As you will see, assessment plays an important role in that process.

MINDFUL ATTENTION AWARENESS SCALE
Day-to-Day Experiences

Instructions: Below is a collection of statements about your everyday experience. Using the 1 to 6 scale below, please indicate how frequently or infrequently you currently have each experience. Please answer according to what *really reflects* your experience rather than what you think your experience should be. Please treat each item separately from every other item.

1	2	3	4	5	6
Almost always	Very frequently	Somewhat frequently	Somewhat infrequently	Very infrequently	Almost never

I could be experiencing some emotion and not be conscious of it until some time later.	1	2	3	4	5	6
I break or spill things because of carelessness, not paying attention, or thinking of something else.	1	2	3	4	5	6
I find it difficult to stay focused on what's happening in the present.	1	2	3	4	5	6
I tend to walk quickly to get where I'm going without paying attention to what I experience along the way.	1	2	3	4	5	6
I tend not to notice feelings of physical tension or discomfort until they really grab my attention.	1	2	3	4	5	6
I forget a person's name almost as soon as I've been told it for the first time.	1	2	3	4	5	6
It seems I am "running on automatic," without much awareness of what I'm doing.	1	2	3	4	5	6
I rush through activities without being really attentive to them.	1	2	3	4	5	6
I get so focused on the goal I want to achieve that I lose touch with what I'm doing right now to get there.	1	2	3	4	5	6
I do jobs or tasks automatically, without being aware of what I'm doing.	1	2	3	4	5	6
I find myself listening to someone with one ear, doing something else at the same time.	1	2	3	4	5	6
I drive places on "automatic pilot" and then wonder why I went there.	1	2	3	4	5	6
I find myself preoccupied with the future or the past.	1	2	3	4	5	6
I find myself doing things without paying attention.	1	2	3	4	5	6
I snack without being aware that I'm eating.	1	2	3	4	5	6

Scoring information

To score the scale, simply compute a mean of the fifteen items. Higher scores reflect higher levels of dispositional mindfulness.

FIVE FACET MINDFULNESS QUESTIONNAIRE

Please rate each of the following statements using the scale provided. Write the number in the blank that best describes *your own opinion* of what is *generally true for you.*

1	2	3	4	5
Never or very rarely true	Rarely true	Sometimes true	Often true	Very often or always true

_____ 1. When I'm walking, I deliberately notice the sensations of my body moving.

_____ 2. I'm good at finding words to describe my feelings.

_____ 3. I criticize myself for having irrational or inappropriate emotions.

_____ 4. I perceive my feelings and emotions without having to react to them.

_____ 5. When I do things, my mind wanders off and I'm easily distracted.

_____ 6. When I take a shower or bath, I stay alert to the sensations of water on my body.

_____ 7. I can easily put my beliefs, opinions, and expectations into words.

_____ 8. I don't pay attention to what I'm doing because I'm daydreaming, worrying, or otherwise distracted.

_____ 9. I watch my feelings without getting lost in them.

_____ 10. I tell myself I shouldn't be feeling the way I'm feeling.

_____ 11. I notice how foods and drinks affect my thoughts, bodily sensations, and emotions.

_____ 12. It's hard for me to find the words to describe what I'm thinking.

_____ 13. I am easily distracted.

_____ 14. I believe some of my thoughts are abnormal or bad and I shouldn't think that way.

_____ 15. I pay attention to sensations, such as the wind in my hair or sun on my face.

_____ 16. I have trouble thinking of the right words to express how I feel about things.

_____ 17. I make judgments about whether my thoughts are good or bad.

_____ 18. I find it difficult to stay focused on what's happening in the present.

_____ 19. When I have distressing thoughts or images, I "step back" and am aware of the thought or image without getting taken over by it.

_____ 20. I pay attention to sounds, such as clocks ticking, birds chirping, or cars passing.

_____ 21. In difficult situations, I can pause without immediately reacting.

_____ 22. When I have a sensation in my body, it's difficult for me to describe it because I can't find the right words.

_____ 23. It seems I am "running on automatic" without much awareness of what I'm doing.

_____ 24. When I have distressing thoughts or images, I feel calm soon after.

_____ 25. I tell myself that I shouldn't be thinking the way I'm thinking.

_____ 26. I notice the smells and aromas of things.

_____ 27. Even when I'm feeling terribly upset, I can find a way to put it into words.

_____ 28. I rush through activities without being really attentive to them.

_____ 29. When I have distressing thoughts or images, I am able just to notice them without reacting.

_____ 30. I think some of my emotions are bad or inappropriate and I shouldn't feel them.

_____ 31. I notice visual elements in art or nature, such as colors, shapes, textures, or patterns of light and shadow.

_____ 32. My natural tendency is to put my experiences into words.

_____ 33. When I have distressing thoughts or images, I just notice them and let them go.

_____ 34. I do jobs or tasks automatically without being aware of what I'm doing.

_____ 35. When I have distressing thoughts or images, I judge myself as good or bad, depending what the thought or image is about.

_____ 36. I pay attention to how my emotions affect my thoughts and behavior.

_____ 37. I can usually describe how I feel at the moment in considerable detail.

_____ 38. I find myself doing things without paying attention.

_____ 39. I disapprove of myself when I have irrational ideas.

Scoring the FFMQ

(Note: R = reverse-scored item)

Observing: Sum responses to items 1, 6, 11, 15, 20, 26, 31, and 36.

Describing: Sum responses to items 2, 7, 12R, 16R, 22R, 27, 32, and 37.

Acting with Awareness: Sum responses to items 5R, 8R, 13R, 18R, 23R, 28R, 34R, and 38R.

Nonjudging of inner experience: Sum responses to items 3R, 10R, 14R, 17R, 25R, 30R, 35R, and 39R.

Nonreactivity to inner experience: Sum responses to items 4, 9, 19, 21, 24, 29, and 33.

TORONTO MINDFULNESS SCALE

Instructions: We are interested in what you just experienced. Below is a list of things that people sometimes experience. Please read each statement. Next to each statement are five choices: "not at all," "a little," "moderately," "quite a bit," and "very much." Please indicate the extent to which you agree with each statement. In other words, how well does the statement describe what you just experienced, just now?

0	1	2	3	4
Not at all	A little	Moderately	Quite a bit	Very Much

1. I experienced myself as separate from my changing thoughts and feelings.

    0   1   2   3   4

2. I was more concerned with being open to my experiences than controlling or changing them.

    0   1   2   3   4

3. I was curious about what I might learn about myself by taking notice of how I react to certain thoughts, feelings, or sensations.

    0   1   2   3   4

4. I experienced my thoughts more as events in my mind than as a necessarily accurate reflection of the way things "really" are.

    0   1   2   3   4

5. I was curious to see what my mind was up to from moment to moment.

    0   1   2   3   4

6. I was curious about each of the thoughts and feelings that I was having.

    0   1   2   3   4

7. I was receptive to observing unpleasant thoughts and feelings without interfering with them.

    0   1   2   3   4

8. I was more invested in just watching my experiences as they arose than in figuring out what they could mean.

| 0 | 1 | 2 | 3 | 4 |

9. I approached each experience by trying to accept it, no matter whether it was pleasant or unpleasant.

| 0 | 1 | 2 | 3 | 4 |

10. I remained curious about the nature of each experience as it arose.

| 0 | 1 | 2 | 3 | 4 |

11. I was aware of my thoughts and feelings without overidentifying with them.

| 0 | 1 | 2 | 3 | 4 |

12. I was curious about my reactions to things.

| 0 | 1 | 2 | 3 | 4 |

13. I was curious about what I might learn about myself by just taking notice of what my attention gets drawn to.

| 0 | 1 | 2 | 3 | 4 |

Scoring

Key: All items were written in the positively keyed direction, so no reverse scoring of items is required.

    Curiosity score: The following items are summed: 3, 5, 6, 10, 12, 13

    Decentering score: The following items are summed: 1, 2, 4, 7, 8, 9, 11

chapter 7

Developing Mindfulness-Based Treatment Protocols

In the previous three chapters, I provided instructions on how to conduct formal and informal mindfulness techniques, and information on assessing mindfulness in clients. In this chapter and chapters 8 and 9, I give you specific information on how to create evidence-based mindfulness interventions for your clients. This chapter describes the evidence-based approach in general, and then outlines a road map for developing mindfulness-based treatment protocols. I also present information on establishing a pre-intervention assessment procedure, choosing clients for mindfulness-based interventions, evaluating treatment progress, and conducting follow-up sessions to improve maintenance of treatment gains. Building on this framework, chapters 8 and 9 will discuss creating protocols for specific populations and problems.

AN EVIDENCE-BASED APPROACH

An evidence-based approach to clinical practice means the approach is informed by research support regarding what is effective in helping people change. From an evidence-based perspective, it's clear that several important aspects of the therapeutic experience must be considered in order to predict what's likely to be effective for your client. The research suggests that several factors are related to client outcomes (Hubble, Duncan, Miller, & Wampold, 2010), including client resources, the therapist-client relationship, intervention strategies and tactics, the client's expectancy of therapeutic outcome, and clinical diagnosis.

Client Resources

Characteristics or conditions, both internal and external, that the client brings to therapy account for up to 40 percent of variance in treatment outcomes (Hubble et al., 2010). What this means is that demographics, personality, genetics, and psychological and behavioral characteristics of clients are among the best indicators of how well clients may do in therapy. Because of the limited research available on how these client resources might impact a client's response to a specific mindfulness-based intervention, you'll have to rely on your clinical skills and experience to help you figure out which mindfulness-based interventions might work best for any given client. While there are limits to what you can do to influence your clients' resources, you can learn what client resources are needed in order for clients to have a successful experience with a mindfulness-based intervention.

An example of how you might screen clients for specific resources can be found in a study that discovered baseline levels of mindfulness were correlated with symptom reduction after participating in a mindfulness-based stress reduction program (Shapiro et al., 2009). The implication of this study is that clients' scores on a mindfulness measure provide a good indicator of how they will respond to mindfulness-based interventions.

An assessment device that I find useful in determining whether my clients are ready for change is the Outcome Rating Scale (ORS), developed by Scott Miller and colleagues (2003). The ORS asks clients to rate how they've been functioning over the past week in four areas on a continuum represented by a 10-centimeter line. The four areas are individually (personal well-being), interpersonally (family and close relationships), socially (work, school, and friendships), and overall (general sense of well-being). You can download the ORS at www.scottdmiller.com by clicking on "Performance Metrics." It's free for your use in private practice; a fee is required for use by an agency, group practice, clinic, or managed behavioral care organization. Scores above 25 generally indicate that clients don't perceive they have significant problems that warrant intervention; thus, they probably won't be motivated to do the work necessary for change. Scores below 25 suggest that clients believe they are having significant difficulties in at least some areas of their functioning; thus, they are more likely to be motivated to change and open to intervention.

Throughout this chapter (and in chapters 8 and 9), I'll point out specific client characteristics or symptoms to assess to help you determine whether a client may respond well to a mindfulness-based intervention or technique. Of course, the research in this area is only just beginning. I hope that in time new research will offer more insight into figuring out who might be a good candidate for a mindfulness-based intervention.

Therapist-Client Relationship

As a therapist, you're already aware that factors such as empathy, respect, genuineness, and warmth are crucial for success. Research confirms this and indicates that the therapist-client relationship accounts for up to 30 percent of variance in treatment outcomes (Sue & Sue, 2008). This is good news, as you can influence this aspect of treatment.

You can improve the therapist-client relationship by asking clients for feedback on how they perceive a session went. Barry Duncan and colleagues (2004) developed the Session Rating Scale (SRS) to do just that. You can give the SRS to clients at the end of the initial interview and at the end of every session thereafter to evaluate their perception of their relationship with you. Clients rate the session on four dimensions that have been found to be predictive of treatment success (Miller, 2009). All items are rated on a continuum. The first rates the relationship from "I did not feel heard, understood, and respected" to "I felt heard, understood, and respected." The second rates the goals and topics from "We did *not* work on or talk about what I wanted to work on and talk about" to "We worked on and talked about what I wanted to work on and talk about." The third rates the approach or method from "The therapist's approach is not a good fit for me" to "The therapist's approach is a good fit for me." And the fourth is an overall rating from "There was something missing in the session today" to "Overall, today's session was right for me" (Duncan et al., 2004). You can download the SRS at www.scottdmiller.com by clicking on "Performance Metrics." It's free for your use in private practice; a fee is required for use by an agency, group practice, clinic, or managed behavioral care organization.

Miller (2009) reports research indicating that initial SRS scores that are very high, 37 to 40, indicate that the client may not feel comfortable with the therapist-client relationship. This may sound counterintuitive; you might think clients who give a very high score to a session must be pleased with the experience. However, very high SRS scores suggest that clients may not feel free to say what they are truly feeling or thinking to the therapist. Scores in this range indicate that clients are not likely to return or remain in therapy for very long. If you have clients with scores in this range, you should ask them for details on how you can improve their experience in the session. Follow-up with appropriate, client-driven changes in the next session, and then ask whether the changes you made were helpful. SRS scores of 36 or less suggest that clients perceive the therapist as someone they can trust and be open with and predict that clients will return for the next session.

Intervention Strategies and Tactics

Interestingly, specific treatment strategies and tactics account for only up to 15 percent of variance in treatment outcomes (Hubble et al., 2010). This makes sense when you consider that client resources and the therapist-client relationship account for up to 70 percent of treatment outcome. However, 15 percent is still a significant amount of variance, and intervention strategies and tactics are something that you, the therapist, can influence. Within an evidence-based approach, you need to choose interventions that are empirically supported. As mentioned, research does support the effectiveness of mindfulness-based approaches for the treatment of several disorders: chronic stress, pain, and illness; anxiety disorders; depression; and eating disorders. In chapter 9, I present specific mindfulness-based protocols for these disorders. Furthermore, there is growing research to suggest that mindfulness-based interventions are probably effective for other disorders.

Faith, Hope, and Expectancy

Another important predictor of how well clients will respond to treatment is their degree of belief in the effectiveness of the treatment and the therapist and their expectations regarding relief of their problems. Clients' faith, hope, and expectancy of the therapist and the intervention account for up to 15 percent of variance in treatment outcomes (Hubble et al., 2010). This data indicates that you should consider clients' opinions about the intervention before implementing a mindfulness-based treatment program. To do so, you can simply ask clients if they think the mindfulness-based technique or program you recommend will be helpful for them. Also ask whether they think they can do the work (with your help).

In order to enhance faith, hope, and expectancy, you must assess your own faith in your ability to deliver the mindfulness-based intervention and your confidence that it will help the client. Your confidence in the intervention will enhance client confidence. The good news about mindfulness-based interventions is that you can tell clients about the growing body of research that supports its effectiveness for a variety of problems. Knowing about this research support will help you present a positive outlook on the effectiveness of this approach for specific clients.

The developers of MBSR and MBCT firmly believe that it's important for therapists to have a mindfulness practice themselves. In chapter 10, I discuss how you can develop and grow in your own mindfulness practice. Your experience with the benefits of mindfulness will help you be more confident in your delivery of a mindfulness-based program using the mindfulness qualities, particularly openness and nonjudging. You might remember that instructions for most mindfulness exercises involve encouraging the client to be open and nonjudging while trying them out. This helps clients feel more comfortable and less threatened by mindfulness exercises, improving their chances of experiencing positive change and healing.

Clinical Diagnosis

Understanding the factors that have been shown to predict treatment success can help you determine how to assess whether a mindfulness-based approach will be beneficial for a specific client. But before you can proceed, you need to determine if the client wants to address specific symptoms, and you must also have an accurate clinical diagnosis. Determining a specific diagnosis will help you decide whether a mindfulness-based intervention is appropriate for the client and will also help you select a specific mindfulness-based approach. Depending on your professional training, you may or may not be able to make a clinical diagnosis. It is beyond the scope of this book to present information and instructions on how to make clinical diagnoses. If you don't have training in clinical diagnostics, you need to refer clients with psychological or behavioral problems for a psychological or psychiatric evaluation. If clients want help coping with pain, chronic illness, or other health and medical problems, you should get permission from their physicians before implementing a mindfulness-based approach.

In chapter 9, I outline protocols for specific problems that have been the focus of mindfulness-based programs: chronic illness, pain, and stress; anxiety disorders; depression; and eating disorders. Before you offer these mindfulness-based interventions to your clients, you must either be qualified to determine whether they meet the criteria for a particular problem or refer them to someone who can determine this for you. Next, I'll discuss pre-intervention assessments. This is the point at which you should determine whether clients need to be evaluated for a specific disorder, either by you or by another professional appropriate for the evaluation.

PRE-INTERVENTION ASSESSMENT

In an evidence-based approach, it's essential to do a pre-intervention assessment to identify client resources, clients' perception of the relationship with you, the problems or issues they're experiencing, and whether they believe the treatment plan will work for them.

You can use the ORS and SRS to determine clients' motivation to change and their perception of the therapeutic relationship. You can also use the ORS to help you and your clients determine specific areas where they would like changes to occur as a result of participating in mindfulness-based therapy. As an alternative to the ORS, you can use any assessment that will generate reliable and valid data on the psychosocial functioning of clients. Examples of measures that provide information on a person's overall functioning, as well as groups of symptoms or disorders, are the Symptom Checklist – 90 – Revised (SCL-90-R; Derogatis, 1992), the Minnesota Multiphasic Personality Inventory – 2 (MMPI-2; Butcher, Dahlstrom, Graham, Tellegen, & Kaemmer, 1989), and the newer Minnesota Multiphasic Personality Inventory – 2 – Revised Form (MMPI-2-RF; Ben-Porath & Tellegen, 2007).

You can administer the FFMQ or the MAAS to get a quantitative measure of clients' initial levels of trait mindfulness. Generally, the higher the score, the more likely it is that clients will benefit from a mindfulness-based approach to therapy. However, because research is still so limited in this area, I wouldn't rule out a mindfulness-based approach for someone with low scores on these tests. You can use scores on mindfulness measures as just one source of information in helping determine whether a mindfulness-based approach might be right for a given client. These tests are also helpful for providing a baseline so that you can assess whether clients' mindfulness scores improve as they develop their mindfulness practice.

RECRUITING CLIENTS FOR MINDFULNESS-BASED INTERVENTIONS

What types of clients are good candidates for mindfulness-based interventions? Based on the information you gather when you conduct the initial interview and assessments, you can make an evidence-based decision. First, does the person desire change? Does he feel like things aren't going well enough in his life? You can assess motivation to change using the ORS or another measure of psychological symptoms or distress. If clients are in distress, they are more likely to be motivated to change and therefore more likely to benefit from a mindfulness-based intervention.

That said, some people who don't have significant problems might be interested in mindfulness-based interventions for preventing problems or for enhancing their current functioning. For example, mindfulness-based interventions for couples are helpful in enhancing marital satisfaction (described further in chapter 8). Mindfulness-based interventions are also used to enhance performance in sports and at work and school.

A second factor to consider is whether clients are willing to devote time to practicing formal and informal mindfulness exercises outside of session. If clients are able to make that commitment, a mindfulness-based approach might be helpful for them.

If you're using a mindfulness-based approach in individual therapy, you can recruit clients who have chronic illness, pain, and stress or those with anxiety disorders, depression or risk for a depressive episode, or eating disorders, particularly binge eating. If you're interested in establishing a mindfulness-based group program for specific disorders, you should recruit six to eight clients who meet the criteria for a specific problem or group of problems. For example you might offer a mindfulness-based group for clients who experience chronic illness and pain and another for those who experience stress and anxiety.

EVALUATING TREATMENT PROGRESS

It's a good idea to give the ORS at the beginning of every session. Clients' scores should show some increase by the sixth session. If a client's ORS scores don't change or if they decrease, you should reassess whether the goals of treatment are appropriate and whether the mindfulness-based approach you are using is fitting. You should also assess the therapist-client relationship. If you make changes in any area of the intervention and the client's ORS scores don't increase within a few sessions, Miller (2009) suggests that you refer the client to someone else.

You can also give the Toronto Mindfulness Scale after you guide clients through a formal mindfulness exercise. Scores on the TMS should increase over time, suggesting that clients are experiencing greater degrees of state mindfulness.

FOLLOW-UP AND MAINTENANCE

Establishing a procedure to follow up on how clients are doing can help you ensure that they maintain the positive changes achieved during treatment. At a client's final session, you can schedule a follow-up session, or a telephone or email follow-up. I recommend a follow-up at one month, then every three months for the first year. In those follow-ups, you can use the ORS to get a quick assessment of whether clients are maintaining their positive changes. If their scores fall below 25, you might suggest they come in for a booster session. In the booster session, you can inquire about what's working for them and what has become problematic, and then help them problem solve. You might also administer the MAAS or the FFMQ to assess whether their trait mindfulness has decreased over time. If their scores have decreased, you can suggest that they devote more time to formal mindfulness exercises, such as sitting meditation or the body scan.

SUMMARY

In this chapter, I presented information on the factors that have the greatest bearing on client outcomes. This will help you develop pre-intervention assessment procedures—a necessary prerequisite so that you'll have the data you need to recruit good candidates for mindfulness-based programs. Once you administer pre-intervention assessments and work with clients to determine what the desired treatment outcomes are, you can select and create a mindfulness-based intervention to fit the client's needs. In the next two chapters I outline specific techniques you should include in treatment protocols depending on the client's resources and problem or desired outcomes.

chapter 8

Protocols for Specific Populations

The mindfulness strategies and techniques that I presented in chapters 4 and 5 are appropriate for general adult populations ages nineteen to sixty-five. However, you might be interested in using mindfulness-based interventions with clients who don't fall into this age range or who don't have the cognitive, psychological, or social functioning to fully engage in typical mindfulness-based techniques. In this chapter, I describe evidence-based mindfulness protocols for children and older adults, and also address using these approaches with couples, since modifications are also needed for clients who fall into this category. As you'll see, most of the mindfulness practices can easily be adapted for these populations.

Mindfulness-based interventions have mostly been used and studied with adult populations. However, clinicians and researchers are beginning to use and study these approaches, in adapted or shortened forms, with children, older adults, and couples, and they are obtaining excellent results. In this chapter, I'll describe clinical adaptations of mindfulness-based interventions for these specific populations and, when available, research support for them. I won't discuss general adult populations, as you can assume that the mindfulness strategies and techniques discussed thus far in this book apply to adults.

CHILDREN AND ADOLESCENTS

Christine Burke (2010) recently wrote about the emerging field of using mindfulness-based approaches with children and adolescents. In her comprehensive research review, she noted that although this field is in its infancy, current research indicates that a core intervention of mindfulness meditation appears to be a promising approach for a variety of pediatric problems. Mindfulness-based interventions have been studied for the treatment of pediatric gastroesophageal reflux, anxiety, attention deficit/hyperactivity disorder, conduct disorder, substance abuse, sleep disorders, mixed psychiatric disorders, and nonclinical groups focused on enhancing health or academic performance. The children studied ranged from four to nineteen years old, with about half being of high school age. Some of the interventions were conducted in school or other community settings. Most of the studies were not randomized controlled trials and used only small samples.

As yet, there isn't enough data to support the idea that mindfulness-based interventions are effective with children and adolescents, but results to date have been positive and I believe we will continue to see research that supports the effectiveness of the approach. Because of the lack of empirical data on using mindfulness-based interventions with youngsters, much of what I present is based on descriptions of what clinical researchers have found helpful, as well as my own clinical experience in working with young people.

Mindfulness-based interventions may be well suited for younger populations, as these approaches tend to incorporate experiential activities such as yoga and walking meditation, which children and adolescents perceive as fun activities. However, psychosocial and developmental factors should be considered when using these interventions. The client's intellectual functioning, ability to attend, language and vocabulary, and physical functioning should inform selection of age-appropriate content and practices. Older children can understand the idea of thinking about one's thinking, which is an integral aspect of the nature of mindfulness. However, there is little research on the best way to present the concept of mindfulness to younger children under age eleven or twelve. With these younger children, you might want to define the concept by way of concrete examples. I describe a few ways to introduce the idea of mindfulness to younger and older children in the section on developmental adaptations.

A key consideration is that younger children have shorter attention spans than adolescents and adults. Length of practices should be adjusted depending on the client's age. In general, five to ten minutes of mindful breathing is suitable for children under twelve, whereas older children can practice for ten to twenty-five minutes. For children under twelve years old, you might start with ten minutes of body scan and five minutes of sitting meditation. From my clinical experience, many children over twelve can handle longer practices. With young clients or older clients with attention problems, you'll have to experiment and shorten the exercises if the client becomes fidgety or loses interest. There is no research available indicating certain lengths of time are more effective for different age groups. These are just suggestions and may be adjusted for individual youngsters depending on their cognitive capabilities and motivation to participate.

Also bear in mind that young people are dependent upon parents and teachers in most areas of their lives and are influenced by peers and siblings. Carefully evaluate these social influences in order to figure out how best to include or address them in your work with a given client. For example, with younger children you might need to get parents to participate along with their children so they can foster mindfulness practices in the home environment and better support the child's development of mindfulness. Similarly, mindfulness-based interventions conducted in schools or other community settings should include teachers and school personnel, at least in terms of helping them understand how to support mindfulness practices in these settings. In the next section I provide some examples of how adults can help support children's growth in mindfulness.

Scheduling Practice

These days, many families have busy schedules, and children often attend day care or participate in extracurricular activities after school. Helping clients and their families set aside time to practice and attend sessions will be critical to the success of the intervention. Preliminary studies of young people suggest that days and duration of practice were related to improved behavior during the course of an intervention (Biegel, Brown, Shapiro, & Schubert, 2009).

Here's an example of how to introduce the practice schedule to clients and their parents.

Therapist: It's important that you and your parents set up a weekly practice schedule for any assignments I give you at the end of each session. Let's talk about your typical schedule during the week and on the weekends. What might be some times when you can practice for about ten to twenty minutes each day? *(Let the child and parents come up with the practice times and write it down for them before you move on.)*

Sometimes it can help you stay motivated if you and your parents can set up some type of reinforcement for practicing. What's something that would help motivate you to stick to your practice schedule? *(Let the child and parents come up with reinforcers for the practice times and write this down for them before you move on. If they need your help in coming up with reinforcers, you could suggest things like playing a game, watching a television program, or receiving a token that the child can trade in for something later on.)*

I'll check in halfway through the week to remind you to practice and see if you have any questions or concerns about your practice. What's the best time to call you during the week to check in? *(You can also send reminder postcards to your clients.)*

Developmental Adaptations

When suggesting a particular mindfulness technique for young clients, you need to demonstrate and guide them through the technique in the office, and then make sure they understand the technique or practice.

Here's an example of how you can check whether young clients understood the directions after you've guided them through a mindfulness exercise.

Therapist: Tell me what you felt when I was asking you to notice your breathing with your eyes closed. *(Let the child describe the experience.)*

Here's an example of how to respond to a problem a child might be having.

Therapist: It sounds like you felt it was difficult to slow your breathing down. Try this: Put one hand on your belly and the other one on the top part of your chest. Now breathe in slowly through your nose and notice your hands moving as your breath moves into your body. When the hand on your stomach moves, just pause and then slowly let the breath out. *(Pause for a moment.)* How did that feel? Were you able to slow down a bit more with your breathing?

Here's an example of how to respond to what worked well for the child.

Therapist: It sounds like you had a good experience with breathing slowly! Can you tell me what you were thinking and feeling when you where trying this exercise?

It's important to help young clients explain to you what they experienced and to give them concrete and specific feedback if they aren't doing the technique correctly. You can also help them make a list of things that might get in the way of their success with home practice, and then come up with strategies to solve these problems. Here's an example.

Therapist: Sometimes when kids practice this at home they might forget the directions, so remember that you can use the CD I made for you to practice the breathing exercise. You might discover other problems in trying to practice at home. For example, it might be hard to find a place and time to practice. What problems do you think you might have when you try to practice this breathing technique at home? *(Explore potential problems with the client and, when appropriate, with parents, and help them come up with solutions.)*

When you come back for your next session, we can talk about what worked and what didn't work. How does that sound? Do you have any other questions for me right now?

The focus of sessions should be on issues or concerns appropriate to the client (Biegel et al., 2009). For younger children this might be school problems, fears, self-regulation of behavior, or getting along with parents, siblings, or peers. Similar issues might arise for adolescents, but for this age group the focus may also be romantic relationships, adjusting to high school, drug and alcohol use, changes in the family, and independence from parents.

CONTENT OF WORDING AND EXAMPLES

When introducing mindfulness techniques, be sure your wording and examples are developmentally appropriate for the age of the client. Using metaphors that clients can identify with will help them generalize what they learn in session to real-life activities. For example, Miles Thompson and Jeremy Gauntlett-Gilbert (2008) use the metaphor of a puppy to help youngsters understand how their minds will wander when practicing mindfulness. The metaphor, originally described by

Jack Kornfield (2003), uses the image of trying to instruct a puppy on how to sit still. Here's how you might present this metaphor in session.

Therapist: Think about a puppy dog that you've watched or played with. The puppy may sit still for a few moments, then it notices something interesting and takes off to check it out. Would you get mad at the puppy? *(Youngsters understand that this is the nature of a puppy and generally say they wouldn't get mad at it.)* Instead of getting mad at the puppy, you might call it back and encourage it to stay and play with you for a few more moments. So you can think about the things that you imagine or feel as being like a puppy dog. During the day, if your thoughts and feelings run away, you can bring yourself back to whatever is happening by taking a breath or two and remembering not to get mad at yourself—just like you would do with a puppy who ran off. Go ahead and try it for a few minutes. Just let your mind wander. *(Pause for two minutes.)* Now take a breath and bring your attention back to where you're sitting and how we're talking together.

Another developmentally appropriate metaphor for how thoughts, feelings, and other reactions can be observed and directed in a gentle and nonjudgmental manner is placing thoughts in bubbles or on a leaf in a stream and watching them float away. As you get to know clients, you might come up with other metaphors that they can relate to. For example, if a client loves horses, you could compare her overwhelming emotions to riding on a runaway horse and explain how coming back to the moment is like slowing the horse down.

Younger clients need you to make the connections for them about how practicing mindfulness might affect their daily life (Thompson & Gauntlet-Gilbert, 2008). Giving examples of what happens when clients are being mindful versus nonmindful might help them understand how to generalize what they're learning in session to their school and home environments. Here's an example.

Therapist: Can you tell me how you've been mindful during the week? *(Pause for a response.)* How has being mindful helped you get along better with your classmates at school? *(You can use other events that the child described here.)* Can you think about something coming up during next week when it might be good to be sure you're paying attention in a happy way?

Also help clients explore the consequences of times when they aren't mindful. Help them take a nonjudgmental look at how they might have been more mindful in those situations. Model an open and honest stance as you discuss possible frustrations, likes, and dislikes regarding the exercises the client has learned.

Therapist: All of us have times when it's hard to pay attention to what's going on around us. When this happens, it can help if you think about it and figure out ways to pay attention without getting mad at yourself. Can you tell me about a time when you weren't being mindful during the week? *(Pause for a response.)* Did not being mindful cause any problems in getting along with your classmates? *(You can use other events that the child described here.)*

Based on interactions with parents and teachers, young people often think there should be a right way to respond, or they fear they aren't doing mindfulness exercises well. Young clients might hesitate to report any problems they're having with the mindfulness techniques. Here is an example of how you might respond to these fears.

Therapist: How are you doing with practicing the meditation exercise I showed you last week? Sometimes kids get concerned that they aren't doing it right. Do you get worried about that? *(Pause for a response, and if the child expresses concern, address the concern right away.)*

The good thing about being mindful is that it helps you remember that everybody makes mistakes. We can learn from our mistakes. If we didn't make mistakes, we might not learn much about ourselves. It's kind of like when you first learn to ride a bike. Do you remember how somebody had to help you at first? And in the beginning, you probably fell a lot. But after falling a few times, you started to notice that if you leaned too far to one side you might fall. So by falling, you learned to ride a bike. You might also have noticed that if you got mad at yourself, it made you fall even more!

To help young clients orient toward mindfulness practice, you can begin each session with the three-minute breathing exercise described in chapter 5. You can also use this exercise periodically during the session to help refocus clients, and again at the end of the session to help them remember how they can use their breath to foster mindfulness during the day.

Tangible rewards can be used to reinforce younger clients when they adhere to their home practice schedule and attend sessions. This will help reinforce their mindfulness practice. Fun stickers or inexpensive prizes such as pencils or a deck of cards make good reinforcements. With teens, you might have to ask them what would be a good reinforcement. In my practice, I've found that teens like coupons for free smoothies.

VARIETY AND REPETITION

To keep young clients involved, it's good to work with a variety of practices, and to improve their mindfulness skills, repetition is important (Thompson & Gauntlett-Gilbert, 2008). Within the session, you can guide clients through a variety of practices, selecting among the body scan, sitting meditation, walking meditation, yoga, and the sensory techniques discussed in chapter 5, which use vision, sound, touch, smell, and mindful eating as stimuli to increase present-moment awareness in an ongoing way.

To help young clients generalize mindfulness to daily activities, you must discuss their daily activities and help them find ways to use these activities as cues to be mindful. For example, teens might use receiving a text message as a cue to pause and tune in to the present moment (Thompson & Gauntlett-Gilbert, 2008). Here's an example of how you might introduce that concept.

> *Therapist:* You mentioned that you use your mobile phone to talk with and text your friends on the weekends and before and after school. You can use your phone to help you be more mindful. Try this: When you get a text message, pause for three breaths. You can use the pause to connect to whatever is going on in your mind and body at that moment. You can think about how you can make a mindful choice in answering the text. What do you think about this idea? *(Pause as your client responds.)* You can still choose to respond to the text, but now you'll be doing it in a way that isn't automatic or unmindful.

Because most young people enjoy music, you could also ask young clients to listen mindfully to different types of music. Other daily activities that might provide a good cue for mindfulness for young people include doing homework, doing chores, playing sports, and talking with friends.

Sample Schedule

In each session, you should guide the client through a variety of experiential exercises and briefly discuss each practice afterward. Here's an example of a session format that would work well for a younger person:

1. **Review.** Review how the homework assignments went for the client. Discuss with the client and, if appropriate, her parents, how the client is doing and any changes or problems that came up since the last session. Discuss being mindful in relation to problems she's encountered. (10 minutes)

2. **Breathing meditation.** Introduce the client to a formal mindful breathing practice (see chapter 4). If parents are also attending the session, have them do the practice as well. (10 minutes)

3. **Discussion.** Discuss how the exercise went and how mindful breathing can help during the day. (5 minutes)

4. **Yoga.** Introduce the client to yoga (see chapter 5). Have the client try a couple of exercises. (15 minutes)

5. **Discussion.** Discuss what the client liked or didn't like about the yoga. (5 minutes)

6. **Homework.** Ask the client to practice the breathing meditation daily for five to ten minutes a day and to do yoga exercises twice a week. Ask her to keep a record of what she practiced each day so that you can review it at the next session. (5 minutes)

Summarizing Approaches for Children and Adolescents

The basic mindfulness techniques to use when developing a mindfulness-based intervention for children or adolescents are the body scan, sitting and walking meditation, yoga, and informal mindfulness during daily activities. I suggested some adaptations, but you may have to make further changes and refinements to fit the individual you're working with. In general, with young clients, using a variety of mindfulness techniques, along with repetition to enhance learning, will be key in helping them develop mindfulness in everyday life. In addition, inviting parents or other important adults to help support young clients' mindfulness practice will increase the likelihood that these clients will grow in mindfulness and reduce their psychological and behavioral problems.

OLDER ADULTS

In an interesting report on using mindfulness with older adults, an elderly client described his experience of a mindfulness-based intervention as "like waking up from a dream" (Smith, 2006, p. 191). With older adults, generally over age sixty-five, you might have to address certain concerns related to aging when conducting mindfulness-based interventions with them, including declining health and cognitive functioning and psychological issues related to self-worth, death, and dying. Although not much research is available that focuses on mindfulness-based interventions specifically for older adults, many of the studies on the effectiveness of mindfulness-based approaches for a variety of disorders have included older adults as participants. However, researchers haven't compared the effectiveness of mindfulness-based interventions between older and younger adults. Therefore, this discussion of applying mindfulness-based interventions to older adults is limited to clinical reports and quasi-experimental studies on adapting mindfulness-based techniques to this population.

Developmental Adaptations

Alastair Smith (2006), a psychologist who conducts group mindfulness-based cognitive therapy with older adults, has found this population to be quite open to trying new techniques. He also notes that many older adults are willing to spend more time on home practice, since they may be retired from work and generally have more time on their hands. Smith found that shortening group sessions from two and a half hours to two hours was helpful if members of the group fatigued easily. A one-hour individual therapy session would be feasible for most older adults, but session length can be shortened for clients who seem to tire before the end of the session.

Smith also suggests using a regular walking speed for walking meditation, rather than the very slow speed generally used for adults. This makes the practice more doable for older clients, particularly those with poor balance or other problems with walking. Indeed, research on walking speed has found that people who have difficulties walking are at higher risk of losing their balance and falling when asked to pay attention to walking very slowly (Gage, Sleik, Polych, McKenzie, &

Brown, 2003). If the client is in a wheelchair or bed bound and cannot walk at all, you can adapt the practice by changing the focus to mindfully moving different parts of the body. You can instruct such clients to slowly move their head, foot, leg, arm, and so on. If clients can't move even this much because of paralysis or other medical issues, you can direct them to imagine moving through a walking sequence.

Because older clients are more likely to have chronic pain and a variety of physical limitations, you might have to modify yoga exercises and sitting positions for meditation. For example, for seated meditation you can instruct older clients to sit on a chair instead of on the floor. Some yoga poses can be attempted in a wheelchair or in bed, and again, those who can't move can still visualize the movements. Remind clients to be gentle with themselves when trying new movements and to use positions that won't cause strain or fatigue.

Helping older clients use mindfulness techniques to embrace negative emotions and physical pain and discomfort can be beneficial, as they often must cope with declining health and physical functioning. Mindfulness meditation, described in detail in chapter 4, can be very helpful to clients in dealing with negative emotions and uncomfortable sensations. Here's an example of how you might introduce mindfulness meditation and its benefits.

> *Therapist:* Mindfulness involves bringing your attention to negative feelings, sensations, and thoughts *(or mention specific symptoms your client is encountering)* with kindness and gentleness. Allow yourself to just observe your experiences. Try not to think too much about a particular experience; rather, just notice it, without judging it. Be open to all of the sensations and feelings you're experiencing right now, in this moment. Take a few minutes to close your eyes or lower your eyelids and notice your inner and outer experiences. *(Pause for 5 minutes.)*
>
> As you broaden your awareness, you'll come to know the temporary and changing nature of these moment-by-moment experiences. In turn, you might find that you feel less anxious or angry or that you experience less pain in response to the current moment. It may help you reduce your perceived pain and encourage confidence in your ability to move your body.

For some older adults, declining cognitive function may interfere with learning the new skills required for mindfulness-based interventions. You might need to screen some older adults for dementia. It is possible to conduct mindfulness-based interventions with clients who might have mild dementia, provided that they have someone at home to remind them and help them practice.

Psychological issues to consider with older adults are concerns about self-worth, death, and dying. In many ways, mindfulness is an excellent approach for helping people work through these issues. Developing the mindfulness qualities of nonjudging and acceptance will help clients strengthen feelings of loving-kindness toward themselves. The loving-kindness meditation described in chapter 4 will help clients foster nonjudging and acceptance of themselves and others.

Mindfulness also encourages a deep understanding of the interconnectedness of all things. Seeing death and dying as existing within this framework of interconnectedness can help older clients appreciate the present moment and process their feelings about death and dying more constructively. Because mindfulness emphasizes being, not doing, it can help older clients focus more on the quality of the present moment than on concerns related to doing and achieving, which may have been important to them earlier in their lives (Rejeski, 2008).

> *Therapist:* As you mature, you have the opportunity to enjoy the present moment as a human being, not a "human doing." Unfortunately, when we're younger we tend to overwork ourselves and overcommit to doing things. You can practice just "being" in a variety of ways, and sitting meditation can help you develop your capacity to simply be with the present moment. Do you think you'd like to try a meditation? *(At this point, you can guide the client through any sitting meditation.)*

Helping Older Clients with Isolation

Some older adults become isolated because they're no longer in work or social environments that provide opportunities for social interaction. You can help improve clients' feelings of social connectedness by discussing ways they can come into contact with others. You can also present isolated clients with the idea that meditation can help them grow in their capacity to feel interconnected with others. This population also typically has more frequent experiences of the death of peers, life partners, and family members and must deal with grief and loneliness as a result. A group format may be particularly helpful for older adults in reducing feelings of isolation. Being able to share their struggles and losses with others going through similar events can help normalize their feelings and help them feel supported.

In describing her work with nursing home resident groups, Lucia McBee (2009) notes that with adaptations for age and physical and cognitive functioning, nursing home residents respond well to mindfulness-based stress reduction. McBee advocates enlisting the assistance of caregivers and health professionals by instructing them on how to support mindfulness practice with these aging adults. For older clients who are homebound, telephone or Web-based approaches have also been used successfully (McBee, 2009; Smith, 2006).

Summarizing Approaches for Older Adults

The basic mindfulness techniques to use when developing a mindfulness-based intervention for older clients include the body scan, sitting and walking meditation, yoga, and informal mindfulness during daily activities. I've suggested several adaptations, but you may have to make further modifications depending on the needs of individual clients. In general, older clients seem to be more responsive to mindfulness-based intervention and to have more time to engage in mindfulness practices than younger adults. And because physical and cognitive limitations often affect this population, mindfulness practice can improve their quality of life. But as with children and adolescents, it may be helpful, even crucial, to enlist the support of caregivers and health professionals in encouraging these clients to practice mindfulness techniques and reminding them to do so.

COUPLES

Mindfulness-based interventions are beginning to be used with couples to improve or enhance their relationship satisfaction. The few approaches described in the research literature have focused on helping couples develop more effective coping and communication skills and reduce negative emotional reactivity toward each other. These approaches have been found to improve communication skills and sexual satisfaction and to lower negative reactivity within the relationship (Carson et al., 2006; Rathus, Cavuoto, & Passarelli, 2006). Because there have been so few studies on this topic, the following discussion of using mindfulness-based approaches with couples is based on clinical descriptions in the research literature and my own experience in using these approaches with couples.

Mindfulness-based relationship enhancement can be conducted with individual couples or in groups of couples. James Carson and colleagues (2006) conduct mindfulness-based relationship enhancement groups, and their approach can be adapted to working with individual couples. They believe that a pre-intervention screening to make sure both partners want to engage in the intervention is critical for therapeutic success. It's also important to make sure the couple understands the time commitment involved in attending sessions and home practice. If the couple has children, it's important to encourage them to set up child care for times when they attend sessions and engage in home practice. Carson and colleagues (2006) found that the number of children a couple had was positively correlated to the likelihood of the couple dropping out of the program. It may be that as child care demands increase, couples have more difficulty finding time to practice and attend sessions.

Most of the mindfulness techniques used for other populations can be used for couples. Loving-kindness meditation and mindfulness meditation may be particularly helpful. In addition, a few unique or specially adapted approaches are helpful here: partner yoga, mindful touch, an eye-gazing exercise, and openhearted discussion.

Loving-Kindness Meditation

Loving-kindness mindfulness meditation should be incorporated early in interventions for couples (Carson et al., 2006). This meditation can be included in the first session to help them remember positive feelings they've had for each other. Once the couple settles into the meditation, instruct them to focus on feelings of loving-kindness toward each other. This will help encourage their acceptance of each other and enhance forgiveness and nonjudging toward self and other. Here's an example of how you might guide couples through this meditation.

Therapist: I'd like to guide you two through a meditation that fosters greater awareness of all feelings you might have for your partner. *(See chapter 4 for instructions on loving-kindness meditation, but modify the practice to focus first on loving-kindness for themselves, then on loving-kindness for the partner.)*

How did that meditation go for each of you? *(Pause and allow both partners to describe their experiences.)*

This meditation can help you two to develop a greater capacity to accept and be more open to each other. When you live with someone, you often develop automatic responses to that person. Being able to stop and not automatically judge what your partner is saying can help improve your connectedness to each other.

Mindfulness Meditation

Individual mindfulness meditation practice can lead to improved partner communication. Growing in awareness and attention can help partners become more attentive to and aware of each other in the present moment. This can encourage honest and open communication, as both partners are able to express themselves more fully while experiencing being listened to by the other. Here's an example of how you might introduce mindfulness meditation to couples.

Therapist: I'd like to guide you two through a meditation that fosters greater awareness of your inner and outer experiences in the present moment. *(See chapter 4 for instructions on mindfulness meditation.)*

How did that meditation go for each of you? *(Pause and allow both partners to describe their experiences.)*

Practicing this type of mindfulness meditation can help you become more aware of what your partner is really saying and doing and reduce destructive automatic emotional responses that you've developed to each other over time. By being more open to whatever is occurring in the present, you're more likely to experience honest and open communication with each other. You'll find that you can express yourself more fully after experiencing being listened to by your partner. You can practice this meditation individually if you like, though some couples enjoy doing sitting meditation together. This might not be possible with your schedules.

Yoga

In working with couples, you can have them practice mindfulness techniques both individually and together. An example of this is to first have them practice yoga poses on their own. Once they have some experience with the poses, you can instruct them to engage in partner versions of yoga (Carson et al., 2006), which involve physically supporting each other when engaging in different yoga poses. Check the resources section of the book for recommended readings on partner versions of yoga.

Mindful Touch Exercise

Encouraging clients to practice mindful touch can help them develop greater physical and sensual intimacy. In the mindful touch exercise, clients are instructed to give each other gentle massages using mindful attention and awareness. After they practice mindful touch, encourage them to consider and discuss how this approach can help improve their physical or sexual relationship.

Start by asking the couple to get in a position in which they can comfortably touch each other. They can sit on the floor on a mat or next to each other on chairs or a sofa.

Therapist: Now that you're sitting comfortably, take a few moments to close your eyes and take a few relaxing breaths. *(Pause for three minutes to allow time for the couple to breathe and relax.)*

Now one of you will mindfully touch and massage the other, and then you'll switch so that each has a turn touching and receiving the touch. Start by gently placing your fingertips on your partner's shoulder and applying soft and gentle pressure *(pause)*. Take the next few minutes to slowly and gently touch your partner's neck, forehead, sides of the face, around the lips, and top of the head. As you touch your partner, notice the sensations on your fingertips. Notice your breath and your partner's breath. Allow yourself to linger on these sensations. If you find your mind wandering, notice this and bring your attention back to the touch. For the one receiving the touch, attend with openness and patience. You might notice a variety of thoughts and feelings arise as your partner touches different parts of your body. Just observe those thoughts and feelings and then bring your attention back to the touch *(Pause for three minutes.)*

Now move to the arms, hands, and fingers. Again, very slowly and gently touch first the right arm, hands, and fingers, and then the left arm, hands and fingers. Remember to attend to the moment in both the receiving and giving of touch. *(Pause for four minutes.)*

Gently place your right hand over your partner's heart and let it rest there for a few moments. *(Pause for one minute.)*

Now move to the legs and feet. Again, very slowly and gently touch first the right leg and foot and then the left leg and foot. Remember to attend to the moment in both the receiving and giving of touch. *(Pause for four minutes.)*

Now both of you take a few conscious, deep breaths, and then switch so that the giver is now the receiver. *(Repeat the above instructions with the other person doing the touch.)*

Again, take a few deep, relaxing breaths. *(Pause for a moment.)*

Let's share your experiences of touching mindfully and receiving the touch. *(Pause and allow both partners to share their experience.)*

How can mindfulness help improve your physical or sexual relationship? *(Allow the couple to share their experiences.)*

You can practice this exercise at home, giving each other a turn to touch and receive.

Eye-Gazing Exercise

Carson and colleagues (2006) describe a technique that they use in their mindfulness-based relationship enhancement program called the eye-gazing exercise. This exercise involves gazing into each other's eyes. For many people, this can feel uncomfortable and stressful, particularly if the other person has hurt them. In the first part of the exercise, the partners gaze into each other's eyes while becoming aware of whatever feelings and thoughts arise and trying not to hold on to or emotionally react to these inner sensations. The second part of the exercise involves continuing to gaze into each other's eyes, but now with the intention of looking for and embracing each other's goodness. Here are instructions for conducting this practice.

Therapist: Please sit comfortably facing each other. You can close your eyes or lower your eyelids. Take three deep breaths. *(Pause for one minute.)*

Now open your eyes and allow yourself to visually explore your partner's face. You might find that thoughts and feelings pop into your awareness. When this happens, bring your attention back to your partner's face. Don't hold on to the thoughts and feelings that arise; simply bring your attention back to your partner's face again and again. *(Pause for three to five minutes.)*

Continue gazing into your partner's face and eyes, but now with the intention of looking for and embracing the goodness in each other. Open yourself to noting positive feelings and thoughts about each other as you gaze at one another with kindness and gentleness. *(Pause for three to five minutes.)*

Let's share your experiences of gazing at your partner. *(Allow the couple to share their experiences.)*

Openhearted Discussion

Carson and colleagues (2006) also include openhearted discussion, based on the Native American council communication model, in their mindfulness-based relationship enhancement program. Openhearted discussion is a council-style group discussion in which couples are instructed to speak from their hearts to each other. Each person is instructed to speak openly, spontaneously, and succinctly about some aspect of himself or herself. Each partner has an opportunity to share thoughts and feelings as the other listens mindfully and without commenting as the person is speaking. Openhearted discussion can also be practiced at home, and through regular practice, couples can learn to reduce negative internal reactions they might have when discussing issues that tend to make them feel angry and anxious. They can do this by paying attention to one another with the intention of extending the mindfulness qualities of nonjudgment and openness not only to each other but toward themselves.

To begin, ask the couple to sit facing each other so they can see each other.

Therapist: Today you'll practice openheartedness with each other. Openheartedness means listening to and receiving something with nonjudgment, patience, and acceptance. I'll ask each of you to share something about yourself. When it's your turn to speak, openly, spontaneously, and succinctly tell your partner about some aspect of yourself. When you're listening, do so respectfully and with an open heart. Observe any negative reactions and judging thoughts as they arise, then bring your attention back to your partner, with openness and interest, as he or she is speaking. Use your breath to help you refocus on your partner.

You might find yourself wondering what you'll say when it's your turn to speak. Again, simply notice these thoughts and, with your breath, bring your attention back to your partner. Simply listen to each other without making comments. *(Ask one partner to begin and to speak for about five minutes. Then ask the second partner to do the same.)*

Couples Retreat

A daylong, mostly silent retreat can help enhance the mindfulness techniques that couples have learned during group or individual couple sessions and can also help couples develop a better understanding of each other. A group format works well for this. Carson and colleagues (2006) conducted this type of group retreat and reported that couples experienced enhanced intimacy during the retreat. Some participants noted surprise at these feelings of interconnectedness, since they hardly spoke to each other during the retreat.

If a group retreat isn't feasible, you can help a couple plan a day to purposely practice several mindfulness activities together. Here's an example of how you might do that.

Therapist: It can be helpful to plan a day, maybe a Saturday or Sunday, when you two can commit to practicing mindfulness together throughout the day. *(If the couple has children, encourage them to get child care for the day or even half a day.)* What would be a good day for you two to schedule a mindfulness day?

Once the couple agrees on a day, help them develop a schedule that incorporates a variety of the formal and informal practices described in chapters 4 and 5. You might encourage them to be silent for some or most of the day.

Summarizing Approaches for Couples

The basic mindfulness techniques to use when developing a mindfulness-based intervention for couples include the body scan, sitting and walking meditation, yoga, and informal mindfulness during daily activities. In general, the focus of mindfulness-based approaches for couples is to develop mindful awareness and attention as the couple interacts moment by moment. The intention to attend with mindfulness during both pleasant and unpleasant interactions will improve or enhance the relationship. Specific adaptations to consider are introducing the loving-kindness meditation in the first session and incorporating partner versions of yoga poses, mindful touch, the eye-gazing exercise, and openhearted discussion. Specific topics to address with couples are physical intimacy, improving communicating skills, and fostering openness and acceptance to help reduce negative reactivity in their interactions.

SUMMARY

In this chapter, I outlined how to adapt mindfulness-based approaches to several specific populations: children, older adults, and couples. The following table summarizes the techniques and adaptations you can use with these populations. Remember that research and clinical work with different populations is new. As you work with clients in these populations, you might find that additional adaptations are necessary. In the next chapter, I present mindfulness-based interventions for particular problems. If you want to use the protocols in chapter 9 with youngsters, older people, or couples, please consider making adaptations recommended in this chapter.

Population	Body Scan	Sitting Meditation	Yoga	Walking Meditation	Mindfulness in Daily Activities	Retreat	Topics
Children (up to age 12)	10 minutes or less	5 minutes or less	Simple poses	5 minutes or less	Examples: games, homework, music, eating, chores	No	Family, peers, fears, self-control, school problems
Adolescents	10 minutes or more	5 minutes or more	Start with simple poses and progress to more advanced as appropriate	5 minutes or more	Examples: texting, homework, music, eating, chores, interacting with friends	No	Family, peers, romantic relationships, adjusting to high school, independence, alcohol or drug use
Older Adults	Yes	Yes	May have to adapt	Yes, with regular walking speed	Examples: eating, recreational activities	Yes	Aging, death, self-worth, pain, illness
Couples	Yes	Yes	Also include partner practice	Yes	Examples: shared activities, partner touch, stressful work and family concerns	Yes	Communication, shared activities, sexuality, parenting

chapter 9

Protocols for Specific Problems

Although mindfulness-based interventions have been used for a variety of problems, there has been more research on the effectiveness of these approaches for some types of problems than others (Baer, 2006). A recent meta-analysis of MBSR suggests that mindfulness-based interventions are effective for a wide range of health and psychological problems (Grossman, Niemann, Schmidt, & Walach, 2004). Of the sixty-four empirical studies found, twenty met criteria for quality and relevance to be included in the meta-analysis. Overall, both controlled and uncontrolled studies showed MBSR to be effective in a wide spectrum of clinical populations with problems such as pain, cancer, heart disease, depression, and anxiety, as well as in nonclinical populations experiencing stress.

I provide information on conducting mindfulness-based interventions for disorders or problems for which enough research has been completed that a mindfulness-based approach is considered effective or probably effective: chronic illness, pain, and stress; anxiety disorders; depression; and eating disorders. Approaches for these problems typically include meditation, the body scan, yoga, and daylong retreats. However, treatment components differ depending on the problem addressed, and special exercises and techniques have been developed for some problems.

The protocols presented in this chapter are a framework for providing a mindfulness-based approach for different problems. Work with your clients to develop an understanding of what mindfulness is by providing a definition of mindfulness and examples of being mindful when you meet with them. Remember to discuss the cognitive and affective qualities of mindfulness as well as the benefits of mindfulness as described in earlier chapters throughout the treatment process.

CHRONIC ILLNESS, PAIN, AND STRESS

In terms of illness, pain, and stress, "chronic" means the person experiences the condition most days of the week for at least six months. Although some people may experience just one of these conditions, illness, pain, and stress tend to occur together. An example might be a person with a spinal injury who experiences pain and stress due to the injury. Mindfulness-based stress reduction has been shown to be helpful for chronic illness, pain, and stress, effectively reducing participants' experience of pain and stress and helping them cope more effectively with illness.

As discussed in chapter 7, before beginning a mindfulness-based intervention it's important to have an accurate diagnosis. In the case of chronic illness and pain, this will entail consulting with the client's health practitioner. In addition to confirming the client's diagnosis, you'll need to obtain the physician's permission for the client to engage in mindfulness practices; you may also need to consult in regard to what practices are appropriate for the client and what modifications may be needed.

Below, I've outlined a typical eight-week protocol that you can use to help you develop a treatment plan for either an individual or a group. In order to help clients develop their mindfulness practice, you'll often need to repeat techniques across sessions. For example, in the protocol below, sessions 3 and 4 repeat the same exercises, as do sessions 5 and 6. This allows you to introduce a technique to clients, have them practice between sessions, and then have them practice it again in the following session. Repeating the exercises in a second session gives you an opportunity to discuss the practice with clients and see how they're responding to the technique.

Session 1

To begin, you'll want to do a pre-intervention assessment to gather data on clients, their presenting problem, and their initial level of mindfulness. This information is key in establishing desired outcomes for individual clients. These assessments will also allow you to establish baseline data for clients so that you can assess their progress through the course of the intervention. After doing the assessments, you can introduce the concept of mindfulness, teach a simple mindfulness practice, and assign homework.

PRE-INTERVENTION ASSESSMENT

Start by administering the Outcome Rating Scale (see chapter 7), and then scoring it with the client. Note areas on the ORS that are in need of improvement; these are possible outcomes of therapy for the client. Here's an example of how you might introduce the ORS.

Therapist: I'll ask you to fill this form out at the beginning of each session. You should see some positive changes in your scores in the first few sessions. If you aren't improving by the sixth session, then our work isn't helping you and we might need to make a change or refer you to someone else.

Next, give the client a measure of chronic pain or coping with illness or stress, such as the McGill Pain Questionnaire (Melzack, 1975), the Social Readjustment Rating Scale (Holmes & Rahe, 1967), or a scale specific to the client's situation that you can give periodically during treatment and follow-up. Depending on the client's situation, you may administer several assessments. Here's how you might introduce the assessment.

> *Therapist:* Since you're concerned about your ability to cope with illness *(pain, stress, or whatever other symptoms your client may have reported)*, this measure will give us important information about changes that should occur as you progress in therapy.

Administer the test and score it right away, then discuss the results with the client and explain the implications. If the client's score is in the nonclinical range, the problem might be something other than illness, pain, and stress and you might have to reassess what the problem is. If the client's score is in the clinical range, whether mild, moderate, or severe, a mindfulness-based approach may be helpful.

Finally, administer a measure of mindfulness in order to establish a reference point so that you can determine whether the client experiences changes in mindfulness during the intervention and at follow-up. You can give the FFMQ or MAAS (see chapter 6). After administering the test, score it with the client and review the result. Here's an example of how you might introduce the mindfulness measure.

> *Therapist:* I'd like you to take a few minutes to complete this questionnaire. It will assess your level of awareness of the present moment. *(Administer the test and score it right away.)* Your score indicates that your current level of mindfulness is *(low, average, high)*.

Based on the client's score, explain what changes in scores are expected over time. Low and average scores should improve over time. A high initial score indicates that the client's score should remain high over time. But do note that for some people with high initial scores, formal mindfulness training might cause their scores to fall at the outset, as they become more aware of how mindless they've been. Over time, their scores will increase again.

INTRODUCING CLIENTS TO MINDFULNESS

Once you've done the pre-intervention assessments, you can introduce clients to the concept of mindfulness and how it will help them reduce their experience of illness, pain, and stress and also help them cope more effectively.

> *Therapist:* A mindfulness-based approach will help you learn how to relax your body and mind. Mindfulness strategies will help you cope more effectively with symptoms of stress, illness, and pain that you experience on a daily basis.

Mindfulness is the practice of attending to your inner and outer experiences moment by moment. It means having the ability to become aware of yourself in any given moment and, in the process, learning how to let go of negative internal and external distractions.

I'll ask you to spend some time each day over the next eight weeks practicing formal mindfulness exercises. I'll also introduce you to informal mindfulness exercises that will help you feel more happiness and joy each day throughout the day.

INTRODUCING MINDFUL BREATHING AND CONCLUDING THE SESSION

To complete the session, introduce clients to breathing meditation, first guiding them through observing the breath, then instructing them in diaphragmatic breathing (see chapter 4). Ask clients to practice observing the breath for ten to fifteen minutes daily. Encourage them to notice when they aren't breathing fully, both during the day and at night, and to practice diaphragmatic breathing for five to six breaths at those times. At the end of the session, administer the Session Rating Scale (see chapter 7) and review the client's responses. If a client gives you a score of 37 or higher, ask the person to reexamine the rating and to give you some feedback on how you can improve the therapy experience.

Session 2

In session 2, you can begin to introduce other mindfulness practices, starting with the body scan. It is helpful for clients to start with the body scan since it's a fairly structured mindfulness practice and can be practiced for a long period of time (forty-five minutes). Initially, clients struggle with mindfulness meditations that aren't as structured, so it's better to introduce those in later sessions, once they've experienced being still using the body scan.

○ **Body scan:** Introduce the body scan (see chapter 4) and guide the client through this exercise. Provide an audio recording to help the client practice the body scan daily between sessions.

○ **Informal mindfulness exercises:** Discuss the idea of practicing mindfulness throughout the day. See chapter 5 for specific exercises. You might want to start with informal mindfulness of breathing and using environmental cues to become more mindful throughout the day, as these are fairly straightforward and effective exercises that can be easily incorporated into anyone's daily routine.

Sessions 3 and 4

Introduce clients to yoga in session 3, once they've had a couple of weeks to practice the body scan and breathing meditations—exercises that involve being still. Yoga provides an active method of helping clients increase their awareness of the mind-body connection. Engaging in gentle yoga can help clients with pain and physical symptoms become kinder and more open toward their body, allowing them to relax more completely into the present moment. With regular practice, yoga will help them increase their physical endurance, flexibility, and strength, which can have a positive impact on their pain and other physical symptoms.

- ○ **Body scan and yoga:** In session 3, introduce clients to yoga exercises (see chapter 5). Ask them to practice the body scan and yoga on alternate days during home practice. In session 4, review their experience with these practices. Guide clients through another body scan in session 4.

- ○ **Informal mindfulness exercises:** Encourage clients to choose at least one type of informal mindfulness practice to engage in each day. Remind them to note whatever they experience internally and externally during these practices.

- ○ **Journaling:** Suggest to clients that it may be beneficial for them to write about their experiences with different mindfulness exercises in a journal. If clients are willing to do this, ask them to bring the journal to session so you can review these experiences together. This will help you develop ideas or suggestions to enhance their mindfulness practice.

Sessions 5 and 6

At this point, you can introduce clients to sitting meditation. Sitting meditation can be difficult for people because it isn't as structured as the body scan and yoga and requires the commitment to sit quietly for longer periods. But by session 5, clients should be more open to trying sitting meditation, as they will have enjoyed the benefits of the body scan and yoga. And although you will initially guide clients through various sitting meditation exercises, these practices provide an avenue for clients to begin taking ownership of their mindfulness practice, especially as they begin to engage in sitting meditation for longer periods without listening to an audio recording for guidance.

- ○ **Sitting meditation:** Guide clients through the lake or mountain meditation or mindfulness meditation (see chapter 4), choosing a different one for each session. You can make an audio recording to give to clients to guide them in practice between sessions. Instruct clients to replace the body scan with sitting meditation and ask that they try to meditate for up to forty-five minutes.

○ **Yoga:** Recommend that clients practice sitting meditation and yoga on alternate days. If a client doesn't feel comfortable doing yoga, suggest doing the body scan instead.

Session 7

By session 7, clients should have good experience with formal and informal practices and feel familiar with them. At this point, you can encourage clients to take ownership of their mindfulness practice. Recommend that they practice mindfulness without audio recordings, as this will foster their ability to cope more effectively with their illness, pain, or other physical symptoms. Suggest to clients that they experiment with different practices and develop a practice schedule that works for them. They can also combine some of the practices. For example, a client could do fifteen minutes of breathing meditation, then thirty minutes of yoga. The next day the client might practice the body scan for thirty minutes, and the following day do mindfulness meditation for thirty minutes and walking meditation for fifteen minutes, and so on. The goal is to help clients develop a routine of formal and informal practice with about thirty to forty-five minutes a day devoted to meditation or a movement practice. This is important for clients with chronic illness, pain, and stress, as it will help them continue to develop the ability to be in the moment and connect with their mind and body in a healthy and adaptive way.

Session 8

In session 8, the final weekly session, you can talk with clients about what has worked for them and areas that they need to continue to be mindful of. You can guide clients through a formal mindfulness exercise and ask them to notice instructions or experiences they haven't noticed before. Tell clients that they can periodically use an audio recording for the body scan, sitting meditation, or yoga instructions to refresh their memory about the practice and deepen their understanding of it. At the end of the session, schedule the first booster session.

Mindfulness Retreat

Clients with chronic illness, pain, and stress can benefit from at least one full-day mindfulness retreat. If you can offer this to your clients, do so. See chapter 3 for details on how to conduct a retreat or refer clients to a retreat experience.

Evaluating Treatment Progress

To evaluate treatment progress, at the end of sessions 4 and 8 administer the same measures of pain, stress, or illness that you gave in session 1. You can also re-administer the FFMQ or MAAS at the end of sessions 4 and 8 to assess changes in mindfulness. You can give the TMS after guiding clients through formal mindfulness exercises to determine their responses to these exercises. Discussing TMS scores might help pinpoint areas of concern that need to be addressed when practicing a particular exercise. Remember to administer the ORS at the beginning of each session and the Session Rating Scale at the end of each session.

Follow-Up and Maintenance

Schedule booster sessions at one, three, and six months after session 8, and schedule a one-year follow-up session. At these sessions, give the same measures of chronic illness, pain, or stress that you administered during the intervention. Also give the ORS and SRS at each booster session, as well as the FFMQ or MAAS. If you guide the client through a formal mindfulness exercise during a booster session, you can also give the TMS afterward. Performance on these measures will help you assess whether clients are continuing to experience positive changes or whether they might need help getting back on track with their mindfulness practice.

ANXIETY DISORDERS

Studies have demonstrated that mindfulness-based stress reduction and mindfulness-based cognitive therapy are both effective in reducing anxiety (Roemer, Salters-Pedneault, & Orsillo, 2006). As discussed in chapter 7, before beginning a mindfulness-based intervention it's important to have an accurate diagnosis. If your client hasn't already received a diagnosis and you aren't qualified to diagnose anxiety disorders, you'll first need to refer the client to a mental health professional who can make the diagnosis.

Once you determine that a client meets the criteria for anxiety problems, you can use the program outlined below to develop a treatment plan suited to the individual client. This program offers a specific evidence-based approach to using a mindfulness-based intervention for anxiety. It isn't as structured as the program for chronic illness, pain, and stress. When working with clients who have anxiety, you need to spend some time educating them about the nature of anxiety in the first session. Then you can introduce mindfulness-based exercises and allow the client to experiment with them.

Clients with anxiety are encouraged to practice a variety of exercises and then choose those that work best for them. They aren't required to devote forty-five minutes to formal practice daily. However, if they want to you should encourage this, since the more they practice, the stronger their mindfulness will become.

Session 1

In session 1, the goal is to gather important baseline data on clients and introduce them to mindfulness. This includes information on overall functioning, anxiety symptoms, level of mindfulness, and perception of the therapeutic alliance. Once you've administered the pre-intervention measures, you'll have more information to guide you in setting up goals for individual clients' needs. Then you can introduce clients to mindfulness, guide them through a simple practice, and assign homework.

PRE-INTERVENTION ASSESSMENT

Start by administering the Outcome Rating Scale (see chapter 7), and then scoring it with the client. Note areas on the ORS that are in need of improvement; these are possible goals of therapy for the client. Here's an example of how you might introduce the ORS.

Therapist: I'll ask you to fill this form out at the beginning of each session. You should see some positive changes in your scores in the first few sessions. If you aren't improving by the sixth session, then our work isn't helping you and we might need to make a change or refer you to someone else.

Next, give the client a measure of anxiety such as the anxiety scale of the Symptom Checklist – 90 – Revised or the Spielberger State-Trait Anxiety Inventory (Spielberger, Gorsuch, & Lushene, 1970). Here's how you might introduce the assessment.

Therapist: Since you're concerned about your anxiety and worry *(you can list other symptoms here that the client may have reported to you)*, this measure will give us important information about changes that should occur in these symptoms as you progress in therapy.

Administer the test and score it right away, then discuss the results with the client and explain the implications. If the client's score is in the nonclinical range, anxiety might not be the problem and you might have to reassess what the problem is. If the client's score is in the clinical range, whether mild, moderate, or severe, a mindfulness-based approach may be helpful.

Finally, administer a measure of mindfulness in order to establish a reference point so that you can determine whether the client experiences changes in mindfulness during the intervention and at follow-up. You can give the FFMQ or MAAS (see chapter 6). After administering the test, score it with the client and review the result. Here's an example of how you might introduce the mindfulness measure.

Therapist: I'd like you to take a few minutes to complete this questionnaire. It will assess your level of awareness of the present moment. *(Administer the test and score it right away.)* Your score indicates that your current level of mindfulness is *(low, average, high).*

Based on the client's score, explain what changes in scores are expected over time. Low and average scores should improve over time. A high initial score indicates that the client's score should remain high over time. But do note that for some people with high initial scores, formal mindfulness training might cause their scores to fall at the outset, as they become more aware of how mindless they've been. Over time, their scores will increase again.

INTRODUCING CLIENTS TO MINDFULNESS

Once you've done the pre-intervention assessments, you can introduce clients to the concept of mindfulness and how it will help them reduce their anxiety symptoms.

Therapist: A mindfulness-based approach to treating anxiety will help you learn how to relax your body and mind. Mindfulness strategies will help you cope more effectively with thoughts, images, and feelings that bother you frequently and increase your anxiety.

Mindfulness is the practice of attending to your inner and outer experiences moment by moment. It means having the ability to become aware of yourself in any given moment and, in the process, to let go of worrisome thoughts and anxiety. Through mindfulness, you can learn what's important to pay attention to, so that when you feel tense or worried you'll have skills to help you follow through on things that might be difficult for you.

PSYCHOEDUCATION ON THE CAUSES OF ANXIETY

Educate the client about the nature of anxiety. Discuss how the sympathetic nervous system responds to threatening situations and thoughts that cause anxious feelings. Explain how anxiety can be a helpful emotion in that it alerts a person to potential problems.

Therapist: Adaptive responses to anxiety involve noticing your feelings of tension and then exploring your response to those feelings. It's also helpful to identify situations and thoughts that might trigger anxiety and tension. Once you learn to recognize anxiety when it's occurring, you can learn strategies that involve mindfulness to help you respond more adaptively to these emotions.

One reason you may worry is to avoid negative emotions. Worry can help you initially feel better and in control, but it isn't adaptive and prevents you from working through your negative feelings. Embracing and being aware of negative feelings through mindful attention and awareness will ultimately help you reduce your overall level of anxiety. By learning how to observe your thoughts and feelings through meditation and other mindfulness practices, you start to view these inner reactions more objectively and react to them in a healthier and calmer way.

INTRODUCING MINDFUL BREATHING AND CONCLUDING THE SESSION

To complete the session, introduce clients to breathing meditation, first guiding them through observing the breath, then instructing them in diaphragmatic breathing (see chapter 4). Ask clients to practice observing the breath for ten to fifteen minutes daily, and encourage them to practice diaphragmatic breathing throughout the day. At the end of the session, administer the Session Rating Scale (see chapter 7) and review the client's responses. If clients give you a score of 37 or higher, ask them to reexamine their rating and to give you some feedback on how you can improve the therapy experience.

Subsequent Sessions

In this protocol, there isn't a set number of sessions for treating anxiety. Use the data you get from evaluating treatment progress (described below) to determine when clients no longer need to see you on a weekly basis.

Your can introduce these clients to formal and informal mindfulness exercises at each session. Guide them through a body scan, sitting meditation, and walking meditation. Ask them to try some yoga exercises at home. Discuss with them what seems to be the most helpful in coping with anxiety. When first introducing clients to a mindfulness exercise, give them an audio recording to practice with at home between sessions.

Encourage clients to take ownership of their mindfulness practice. Suggest that they experiment with different mindfulness practices and develop a practice schedule that works for them. They can also combine practices. For example, a client could do ten minutes of breathing meditation, then thirty minutes of yoga. The next day the client might practice the body scan for thirty minutes, and the following day do a mindfulness meditation for thirty minutes and walking meditation for fifteen minutes, and so on. The goal is to help clients develop a routine of formal and informal mindfulness practice that works for them. This will help them continue to develop the ability to be in the moment and connect with their mind and body in a healthy and adaptive manner. Once clients have become familiar with a mindfulness exercise, recommend that they practice that exercise without an audio recording, as this will help foster self-regulation.

Specific informal practices recommended for these clients are observing and describing, mindfulness in daily activities, and yoga. Recommended formal practices are the body scan and sitting meditation. Guide these clients through breathing practices, mindfulness meditation, and the lake or mountain meditation. The mountain meditation may be particularly helpful for clients with anxiety, as the image of the solidness of the mountain helps foster calmness in the midst of everyday stress.

Also suggest to these clients that it may be beneficial for them to write about their experiences with different mindfulness exercises in a journal. If clients are willing to do this, ask them to bring the journal to session so you can review these experiences together. This will help you develop ideas or suggestions to enhance their mindfulness practice.

Final Session

Once clients have made significant improvement in coping with anxious feelings, they need no longer come for weekly sessions. At the final weekly session, talk with clients about what has worked for them and areas that they need to continue to be mindful of. You can guide clients through a formal mindfulness exercise and ask them to notice instructions or experiences they haven't noticed before. Tell clients that they can periodically use an audio recording for the body scan, sitting meditation, or yoga instructions to refresh their memory about the practice and deepen their understanding of it. At the end of the session, schedule the first booster session.

Evaluating Treatment Progress

To evaluate treatment progress, about midway through treatment and at the last session administer the same pre-intervention measure of anxiety that you gave in session 1. At these points you can also re-administer the FFMQ or MAAS to assess changes in mindfulness. You can give the TMS after guiding clients through formal mindfulness exercises to determine their responses to these exercises. Discussing TMS scores might help pinpoint areas of concern that need to be addressed when practicing a particular exercise. Remember to administer the ORS at the beginning of each session and the SRS at the end of each session.

Follow-Up and Maintenance

Schedule booster sessions for one, three, and six months after the final session, and schedule a one-year follow-up session. At these sessions give the same measure of anxiety that you administered during the intervention. Also give the ORS and SRS at each booster session, as well as the FFMQ or MAAS. If you guide the client through a formal mindfulness exercise during a booster session, you can also give the TMS afterward. Performance on these measures will help you assess whether clients are continuing to experience positive changes or whether they might need help getting back on track with their mindfulness practice.

DEPRESSION

Mindfulness-based approaches have been shown to be particularly helpful for preventing *relapse* of depression (Coffman et al., 2006), and some researchers have suggested that these approaches may be helpful for treating depression when first diagnosed, as well (Barnhofer & Crane, 2006). As discussed in chapter 7, before beginning a mindfulness-based intervention it's important to have an accurate diagnosis. If your client hasn't already received a diagnosis and you aren't qualified to diagnose depression, you'll first need to refer the client to a mental health professional who can make the diagnosis.

Once you determine that a client meets the criteria for depression or for preventing depression relapse, you can use the program outlined below to develop a treatment plan suited to the individual client. As with integrating mindfulness into therapy for anxiety, the mindfulness-based approach for depression outlined below isn't as structured as the program outlined for treating chronic illness, pain, and stress.

With clients who are depressed or at risk for depression, it's important to provide psychoeducation about depression. People who are depressed tend to have more sadness and anger than those who aren't depressed. They tend to be less physically active and have disordered sleep, sleeping too little or too much. Depression can affect all aspects of a person's ability to enjoy the moment, including eating, relaxing, and sexuality. A mindfulness-based approach will help these clients expand their awareness beyond their negative internal experiences and allow them to attend to and appreciate aspects of life that they've lost contact with.

Clients with depression or at risk for depression are encouraged to practice a variety of exercises and then choose those that work best for them. They aren't required to devote forty-five minutes to formal practice daily. However, if they want to you should encourage this, since the more they practice, the stronger their mindfulness will become.

Session 1

As with all of the protocols outlined in this chapter, in session 1 it's important to first administer pre-intervention assessments. Then you can move to psychoeducation on depression and introducing the concept of mindfulness. In the suggested script below, psychoeducation on depression is integrated into introducing the concept of mindfulness.

PRE-INTERVENTION ASSESSMENT

Start by administering the Outcome Rating Scale (see chapter 7), and then scoring it with the client. Note areas on the ORS that are in need of improvement; these are possible goals of therapy for the client. Here's an example of how you might introduce the ORS.

Therapist: I'll ask you to fill this form out at the beginning of each session. You should see some positive changes in your scores in the first few sessions. If you aren't improving by the sixth session, then our work isn't helping you and we might need to make a change or refer you to someone else.

Next, give the client a measure of depression, such as the depression scale of the Symptom Checklist – 90 – Revised or the Beck Depression Inventory – II (Beck, Steer, & Brown, 1996). Here's how you might introduce the assessment.

Therapist: Since you're concerned about depression (*you can list other symptoms here that the client may have reported to you*), this measure will give us important information about changes that should occur in these symptoms as you progress in therapy.

Administer the test and score it right away, then discuss the results with the client and explain the implications. If the client's score is in the nonclinical range, depression might not be the problem and you might have to reassess what the problem is. If the client's score is in the clinical range, whether mild, moderate or severe, a mindfulness-based approach may be helpful.

Finally, administer a measure of mindfulness in order to establish a reference point so that you can determine whether the client experiences changes in mindfulness during the intervention and at follow-up. You can give the FFMQ or MAAS (see chapter 6). After administering the test, score it with the client and review the result. Here's an example of how you might introduce the mindfulness measure.

> *Therapist:* I'd like you to take a few minutes to complete this questionnaire. It will assess your level of awareness of the present moment. *(Administer the test and score it right away.)* Your score indicates that your level of mindfulness is currently *(low, average, high).*

Based on the client's score, explain what changes in scores are expected over time. Low and average scores should improve over time. A high initial score indicates that the client's score should remain high over time. But do note that for some people with high initial scores, formal mindfulness training might cause their scores to fall at the outset, as they become more aware of how mindless they've been. Over time, their scores will increase again.

INTRODUCING CLIENTS TO MINDFULNESS AND PSYCHOEDUCATION ON DEPRESSION

Once you've done the pre-intervention assessments, you can introduce clients to the concept of mindfulness and how it will help them reduce symptoms of depression or lower their risk of relapse.

> *Therapist:* A mindfulness-based approach will help you learn how to feel better about yourself, the future, and the world around you. Mindfulness strategies will help you cope more effectively with thoughts and feelings that promote symptoms of depression. When people become depressed, they tend to be more aware of negative thoughts about themselves, other people, and the future. They lose awareness of the present moment and of positive events in their lives. They find it difficult to stop thinking about these negative thoughts and often ruminate about them. Ruminating leads to sadness and despair.
>
> Everyone experiences feelings of sadness and loss. These feelings are natural and part of being human. Mindfulness offers you a new awareness of these feelings and helps you not become overwhelmed by them. If you've had a depressive episode before and are now doing okay, when you experience feelings of sadness you might feel afraid that you'll experience another depressive episode. This kind of anticipation about getting depressed again

might trigger negative thoughts and rumination, which can eventually lead to depression.

Mindfulness is the practice of attending to your inner and outer experiences moment by moment. It means having the ability to become aware of yourself in any given moment and, in the process, to let go of worrisome thoughts and negative feelings. Mindfulness can help lift you into a new awareness of yourself so that you can begin to work through your negative feelings and thoughts without becoming depressed.

During the time we're working together, I'll ask you to spend some time each day practicing formal mindfulness exercises. I'll also introduce you to informal mindfulness exercises that will help you feel more happiness and joy each day throughout the day.

INTRODUCING MINDFUL BREATHING AND CONCLUDING THE SESSION

To complete the session, introduce clients to breathing meditation, first guiding them through observing the breath, then instructing them in diaphragmatic breathing (see chapter 4). Ask clients to practice observing the breath for ten to fifteen minutes daily, and encourage them to practice diaphragmatic breathing throughout the day. At the end of the session, administer the Session Rating Scale (see chapter 7) and review the client's responses. If a client gives you a score of 37 or higher, ask the person to reexamine the rating and to give you some feedback on how you can improve the therapy experience.

Subsequent Sessions

In this protocol, there isn't a set number of sessions for treating depression. Use the data you get from evaluating treatment progress (described below) to determine when clients no longer need to see you on a weekly basis.

Your can introduce these clients to formal and informal mindfulness exercises at each session. Guide them through a body scan, sitting meditation, and walking meditation. Ask them to try some yoga exercises at home. Discuss with them what seems to be the most helpful in coping with depression. When first introducing clients to a mindfulness exercise, give them an audio recording to practice with at home between sessions.

People who are depressed are usually physically inactive. Encourage these clients to engage in some type of movement for at least thirty minutes each day. This can include mindfulness practices such as yoga or walking meditation, or other forms of exercise or normal walking.

Encourage clients to take ownership of their mindfulness practice. Suggest that they experiment with different mindfulness practices and develop a practice schedule that works for them. They can combine some of these mindfulness practices. For example, a client could do ten minutes of breathing meditation, then thirty minutes of yoga. The next day the client might practice the body scan for thirty minutes, and the following day do a mindfulness meditation for thirty minutes and walking meditation for fifteen minutes, and so on. The goal is to help clients develop a routine of formal and informal mindfulness practice that works for them. This will help them continue to develop the ability to be in the moment and connect with their mind and body in a healthy and adaptive manner. Once clients have become familiar with a mindfulness exercise, recommend that they practice that exercise without an audio recording, as this will help foster self-regulation.

Specific informal practices recommended for these clients are yoga, observing and describing, and mindfulness in daily activities. Informal practices are particularly helpful for these clients, so introduce a different informal practice at each session. All of these practices can help depressed clients notice pleasant inner and outer experiences throughout the day that they otherwise may tend to ignore. It will also help them become more aware of "being," rather than just "doing." With observing and describing, discuss how they can use this practice to cope with negative thoughts about themselves, others, and the future.

Specific formal practices recommended for these clients are the body scan and sitting meditation. Guide these clients through the lake and mountain meditations and loving-kindness meditation in different sessions. Loving-kindness meditation may be particularly helpful for people at risk of depression, as it helps soften the heart and decrease negative feelings toward themselves and those who may have hurt them.

Also suggest to these clients that it may be beneficial for them to write about their experiences with different mindfulness exercises in a journal. If clients are willing to do this, ask them to bring the journal to session so you can review these experiences together. This will help you develop ideas or suggestions to enhance their mindfulness practice.

Final Session

Once clients have made significant improvement in coping with feelings of sadness and negativity, they need no longer come for weekly sessions. At the final weekly session, talk with clients about what has worked for them and areas that they need to continue to be mindful of. You can guide clients through a formal mindfulness exercise and ask them to notice instructions or experiences they haven't noticed before. Tell clients that they can periodically use an audio recording for the body scan, sitting meditation, or yoga instructions to refresh their memory about the practice and deepen their understanding of it. At the end of the session, schedule the first booster session.

Evaluating Treatment Progress

To evaluate treatment progress, about midway through treatment and at the last session. administer the same pre-intervention measure of depression that you gave in session 1. At these points you can also re-administer the FFMQ or MAAS to assess changes in mindfulness. You can give the TMS after guiding clients through formal mindfulness exercises to determine their responses to these exercises. Discussing TMS scores might help pinpoint areas of concern that need to be addressed when practicing a particular exercise. Remember to administer the ORS at the beginning of each session and the SRS at the end of each session.

Follow-Up and Maintenance

Schedule booster sessions for one, three, and six months after the final session, and also schedule a one-year follow-up session. At these sessions give the same measure of depression that you administered during the intervention. Also give the ORS and SRS at each booster session, as well as the FFMQ or MAAS. If you guide the client through a formal mindfulness exercise during a booster session, you can also give the TMS afterward. Performance on these measures will help you assess whether clients are continuing to experience positive changes or whether they might need help getting back on track with their mindfulness practice.

EATING DISORDERS

Eating disorders that have been shown to respond to a mindfulness-based approach include bulimia and binge eating related to obesity (Kristeller et al., 2006). As discussed in chapter 7, before beginning a mindfulness-based intervention it's important to have an accurate diagnosis. If your client hasn't already received a diagnosis and you aren't qualified to diagnose eating disorders, you'll first need to refer the client to someone who can make the diagnosis.

Below, I've outlined a typical eight-week protocol that you can use to help develop a treatment plan for either an individual or a group.

Session 1

As with all of the protocols outlined in this chapter, in session 1 it's important to first administer pre-intervention assessments. Then you can move on to introducing the concept of mindfulness.

PRE-INTERVENTION ASSESSMENT

Start by administering the Outcome Rating Scale (see chapter 7), and then scoring it with the client. Note areas on the ORS that are in need of improvement; these are possible goals of therapy for the client. Here's an example of how you might introduce the ORS.

Therapist: I'll ask you to fill this form out at the beginning of each session. You should see some positive changes in your scores in the first few sessions. If you aren't improving by the sixth session, then our work isn't helping you and we might need to make a change or refer you to someone else.

Next, give the client a measure of eating problems, such as the Eating Disorder Inventory – 3 (EDI-3; Gardner, 2004).

> *Therapist:* Since you're concerned about your ability to eat in a healthy way *(you can list other symptoms here that your client may have reported to you)*, this measure will give us important information about changes that should occur as you progress in therapy.

Administer the test and score it right away, then discuss the results with the client and explain the implications. If the client's score is in the nonclinical range, eating might not be the problem and you might have to reassess what the problem is. If the client's score is in the clinical range, whether mild, moderate or severe, a mindfulness-based approach may be helpful.

Finally, administer a measure of mindfulness in order to establish a reference point so that you can determine whether the client experiences changes in mindfulness during the intervention and at follow-up. You can give the FFMQ or MAAS (see chapter 6). After administering the test, score it with the client and review the result. Here's an example of how you might introduce the mindfulness measure.

> *Therapist:* I'd like you to take a few minutes to complete this questionnaire. It will assesses your level of awareness of the present moment. *(Administer the test and score it right away.)* Your score indicates that your level of mindfulness is currently *(low, average, high)*.

Based on the client's score, explain what changes in scores are expected over time. Low and average scores should improve over time. A high initial score indicates that the client's score should remain high over time. But do note that for some people with high initial scores, formal mindfulness training might cause their scores to fall at the outset, as they become more aware of how mindless they've been. Over time, their scores will increase again.

INTRODUCING CLIENTS TO MINDFULNESS

Once you've done the pre-intervention assessments, you can introduce clients to the concept of mindfulness and how it will help them reduce their problematic eating behavior and also help them cope more effectively with emotions and thoughts that lead to overeating.

> *Therapist:* A mindfulness-based approach will help you learn how to become more mindful of your body's nutritional and physical needs so that you can respond with adaptive eating behaviors. Mindfulness strategies will help you cope more effectively with thoughts and feelings that you experience on a daily basis that get in the way of you eating well and exercising.
>
> Mindfulness is the practice of attending to your inner and outer experiences moment by moment. It means having the ability to become aware of

yourself in any given moment and, in the process, learning how to let go of negative internal and external distractions.

I'll ask you to spend some time each day over the next eight weeks practicing formal mindfulness exercises. I'll also introduce you to informal mindfulness exercises that will help you feel more happiness and joy each day throughout the day.

INTRODUCING MINDFUL BREATHING AND CONCLUDING THE SESSION

To complete the session, introduce clients to breathing meditation, first guiding them through observing the breath, then instructing them in diaphragmatic breathing (see chapter 4). Ask clients to practice observing the breath for ten to fifteen minutes daily, and encourage them to practice diaphragmatic breathing throughout the day. At the end of the session, administer the Session Rating Scale (see chapter 7) and review the client's responses. If clients give you a score of 37 or higher, ask them to reexamine their rating and to give you some feedback on how you can improve the therapy experience.

Session 2

In session 2, you can begin to introduce other mindfulness practices, specifically mindful eating and the body scan. It is helpful for clients to start with the body scan since it's a fairly structured mindfulness practice and can be practiced for a long period (forty-five minutes). The body scan will help these clients develop a kinder and more open body awareness. Often, people with eating disorders aren't accepting of how their body feels and looks. The body scan offers them a method to embrace their body nonjudgmentally and with loving-kindness.

It's also important to introduce mindful eating early on in the intervention since these clients have difficulty interacting with food in a positive and healthy way. Mindful eating will help these clients slow down and savor and appreciate their food. It can also help them become more aware of when they are full and allow them to decrease or increase their food intake as appropriate. In addition, practicing mindful eating will help these clients become aware of negative feelings, images, and thoughts regarding eating and food so that they can learn to let them go. This will help them begin to develop appreciation for food and foster healthier feelings, images, and thoughts about eating.

- **Mindful eating:** Introduce mindful eating (see chapter 5) and guide clients through this practice.

- **Body scan:** Introduce the body scan (see chapter 4) and guide clients through this exercise. Provide an audio recording to help them practice the body scan daily between sessions.

○ **Homework:** Instruct clients to eat one snack or meal per day mindfully.

○ **Journaling:** Suggest to clients that it may be beneficial for them to write about their experiences with different mindfulness exercises in a journal. If clients are willing to do this, ask them to bring the journal to session so you can review these experiences together. This will help you develop ideas or suggestions to enhance their mindfulness practice.

Session 3

Ask clients to talk about potential triggers that make them feel like they want to eat when they aren't hungry and that might lead to overeating. Encourage them to think about internal experiences, such as emotions or specific thoughts, and external experiences, such as particular situations, that might trigger overeating. An example of an internal trigger might be feelings of stress; an external trigger might be going to a party. Ask clients to describe some of these triggers. Once they can identify one or two triggers, you can guide them through a binge trigger meditation.

○ **Binge trigger meditation:** Guide clients through a mindfulness meditation (see chapter 4) with a specific focus on noticing feelings, thoughts, and images of the binge-eating triggers identified in the preceding discussion. Have clients note these triggers as they arise in their consciousness. Provide an audio recording to help the client practice between sessions.

○ **Mindful eating:** Repeat the mindful eating exercise, this time using some other type of food as focus point—something that's a potential binge trigger for the client.

○ **Homework**: Instruct clients to do a three- to five-minute breathing meditation before one meal each day or when they notice a potential binge-eating trigger.

Session 4

Clients who binge often do so when they aren't hungry. Building on the discussion in session 3, about how internal and external experiences trigger the desire to eat and lead to bingeing, in session 4 you can discuss hunger cues so clients can become more aware of the physiological sensations and psychological experiences associated with the need to nourish the body. These might include sensations in the stomach indicating the beginning of hunger and feeling distracted from work because blood sugar is dropping due to lack of food. After discussing hunger cues, you can guide clients through a hunger meditation.

○ **Hunger meditation:** Guide clients through a mindfulness meditation, this time with a focus on feelings, thoughts, and images of physiological hunger. Have clients note these experiences as they arise in their consciousness. Provide an audio recording to help them practice between sessions.

- ○ **Mindful eating:** Repeat the mindful eating exercise, again using some other type of food as focus point. Once again, choose a food item that's a potential binge-eating trigger.

- ○ **Mindful food choices:** Discuss being more mindful of the types of food the client chooses. Use several examples, such as choosing between cookies and an apple, or pizza and a salad, and help clients use breathing and mindful awareness to consider each item and then choose what they truly want to eat.

- ○ **Homework:** Instruct clients to practice waiting until they feel physically hungry before eating, for at least one meal each day. Also ask them to practice mindful awareness of making a choice between two foods each day.

Sessions 5 and 6

Clients who binge often aren't aware of what they're tasting and when they become full. Continue to build on the discussions of binge triggers and sensations of hunger in previous sessions. In session 5, discuss mindfully tasting and tuning in to satiety cues to help clients become aware of the physiological sensations and psychological experiences associated with having eaten enough food. These might include sensations of the beginning of fullness in the stomach and changes in the taste of the food. As clients eat mindfully, these sensations can help them stop eating when they've consumed enough to nourish the body. At this point, you can guide clients through a taste and satiety meditation. Encourage them to linger over their food, noticing the smells, flavors, and textures of the food and the environment in which they're eating. In session 6, review what they experienced in regard to feelings of satiety and taste between sessions.

- ○ **Taste and satiety meditation:** In both sessions 5 and 6, guide clients through a mindfulness meditation with a focus on feelings, thoughts, and images of satiety and taste. Have them note these experiences as they arise into their consciousness. Provide an audio recording to help them practice between sessions.

- ○ **Yoga:** In session 5, introduce clients to yoga (see chapter 5) and ask them to practice yoga at least twice before session 6. In session 6, ask how the yoga practice went.

- ○ **Homework:** Ask clients to attend to taste and satisfaction or enjoyment for at least one meal each day, and to stop eating when moderately full. For homework after session 6, ask clients to eat at a buffet once before the next session while practicing mindful awareness of food choices, taste, and satiety.

Session 7

Clients who binge will have days when they relapse and then will feel angry at themselves for eating too much. This anger generally causes them to restrict their food intake, which eventually leads to another binge. Loving-kindness meditation can help these clients begin to accept and forgive themselves for overeating. Explain that mindfulness practice will help them develop a balanced approach to eating and inner wisdom about honoring and responding to their nutritional and physical needs. Ask these clients to identify thoughts and feelings that they notice when they eat too much. Discuss how these thoughts and feelings are temporary and don't define them as a person—even feelings of self-loathing or guilt.

- **Walking meditation:** Introduce walking meditation (see chapter 4) and guide clients through the exercise. Provide an audio recording to help them practice between sessions.

- **Loving-kindness meditation:** Introduce loving-kindness meditation (see chapter 4) and guide clients through this exercise. Provide an audio recording to help them practice between sessions.

- **Homework:** Ask clients to alternate their practice of mindful walking, yoga, and loving-kindness meditation from day to day. Also instruct them to eat all meals and snacks mindfully.

Session 8

In session 8, the final weekly sessions, you can talk with clients about what has worked for them and areas that they need to continue to be mindful of. Discuss changes made, future goals, and relapse prevention. If you're working with a group, you can close this session with a celebratory potluck meal. With an individual client, you can provide a simple meal or a celebratory dessert to share together. This celebratory food reflects the idea of being able to appreciate and be grateful for what is present in the moment. In this situation, it can be the understanding that clients have learned healthier and more adaptive ways to nourish themselves by growing in mindfulness over the course of the last two months.

You can guide clients through a formal mindfulness exercise and ask them to notice instructions or experiences they haven't noticed before. Tell clients that they can periodically use an audio recording for the body scan, sitting meditation, or yoga instructions to refresh their memory about the practice and deepen their understanding of it. At the end of the session, schedule the first booster session.

Evaluating Treatment Progress

To evaluate treatment progress, at the end of sessions 4 and 8 administer the same pre-intervention measure of eating problems that you gave in session 1. You can also re-administer the FFMQ or MAAS at the end of sessions 4 and 8 to assess changes in mindfulness. You can give the TMS after guiding clients through formal mindfulness exercises to determine their responses to these exercises. Discussing TMS scores might help pinpoint areas of concern that need to be addressed when practicing a particular exercise. Remember to administer the ORS at the beginning of each session and the SRS at the end of each session.

Follow-Up and Maintenance

Schedule booster sessions at one, three, and six months after session 8, and schedule a one-year follow-up session. At these sessions, give the same measure of eating problems that you administered during the intervention. Also give the ORS and SRS at each booster session, as well as the FFMQ or MAAS. If you guide the client through a formal mindfulness exercise during a booster session, you can also give the TMS afterward. Performance on these measures will help you assess whether clients are continuing to experience positive changes or whether they might need help getting back on track with their mindfulness practice.

SUMMARY

The protocols presented in this chapter provide guidelines for using mindfulness-based interventions to treat chronic illness, pain, and stress; anxiety disorders; depression; and certain eating disorders. As you've seen, assessment of the client's symptoms, mindfulness, and perception of the therapeutic experience are a major element in these protocols. Using assessment in this way will help you build an evidence-based practice—and evidence-based interventions for individual clients.

Up to this point in the book, I've provided information to help you develop and present mindfulness-based interventions for individual clients. However, as mentioned, in order to deliver these interventions effectively, it's important for therapists to have their own mindfulness practice. So in the next chapter, I'll present information on just that: how to develop your own mindfulness practice.

chapter 10

Therapist Training in Mindfulness

As a therapist you know the importance of self-care, but do you practice self-care on a regular basis? Research has consistently shown that health professionals are at risk for developing the same psychological and health problems that their patients have (Shapiro & Carlson, 2009). You may feel that you're too busy helping others to take the time to tend to your own needs and deal with the stress that occurs not only at work, but in your personal life as well.

As discussed throughout this book and particularly in chapter 2, practicing mindfulness has many benefits—psychological, physiological, social, and spiritual. This alone would be good reason to develop your own practice. Further, Jon Kabat-Zinn and other experts in the field of mindfulness-based interventions believe that in order to be an effective teacher of mindfulness, you must first develop your own mindfulness practice (Baer, 2006; Kabat-Zinn, 1990, 2005).

Hopefully this book has already given you a good idea of how to develop your own practice and become more mindful. In this chapter, I'll provide more suggestions on how you, as a therapist, can incorporate mindfulness into your daily life, including your professional activities and work settings.

RESEARCH ON THE BENEFITS OF THERAPIST MINDFULNESS

Recent studies have consistently demonstrated that mindfulness-based interventions can improve many aspects of therapists' functioning (Shapiro & Carlson, 2009). Most of these studies have evaluated programs with therapists in training as participants; only a few have studied practicing mental health care professionals. Mindfulness practices used in these studies have included the body scan, walking meditation, sitting meditation (including loving-kindness meditation), yoga, and other informal mindfulness practices. Some of the programs include didactic sessions on theories of mindfulness and research support for mindfulness-based programs (Christopher, Christopher, Dunnagan, & Schure, 2006). Examples of specific benefits therapists reported after participating in mindfulness-based programs include reductions in anxiety, stress, and rumination, and increases in self-compassion, positive emotions, and empathy.

Studies evaluating the effects of these programs have focused on outcomes for the participants, meaning they evaluated only how participants improved in psychosocial functioning. A handful of studies have begun to examine whether therapists who are higher in trait mindfulness or who have received training in mindfulness have better outcomes with their clients than those with lower trait mindfulness or no training in mindfulness (Stanley et al., 2006). My review of the research literature suggests that the jury is still out on this question. The results are mixed, with some studies showing no difference between therapists lower or higher in mindfulness, some showing a positive correlation between therapist mindfulness and client outcomes, and others showing a negative correlation.

Even so, from an evidence-based perspective you can feel confident that increasing your mindfulness will improve your psychosocial functioning and help prevent burnout. And therapists who practice mindfulness believe that their practice helps them be more compassionate and nonjudgmental with clients (Christopher et al., 2006). These characteristics can improve the therapist-client relationship, and as discussed in chapter 7, this relationship accounts for up to 30 percent of variance in client outcomes (Sue & Sue, 2008). With these positives in mind, let's examine how you can incorporate mindfulness into your personal and professional life.

INCORPORATING MINDFULNESS INTO YOUR PERSONAL LIFE

There are many opportunities to take continuing education workshops on mindfulness, and some mindfulness centers offer mindfulness training specifically for professionals. For example, the University of Massachusetts Medical School's Center for Mindfulness in Medicine, Health Care, and Society, in Worcester, conducts a yearly scientific and clinical conference on mindfulness and offers courses and supervision throughout the year for those who wish to be certified by the center. I've found that attending at least one mindfulness conference a year helps foster both my mindfulness-based clinical practice and my own personal mindfulness practice. I live on the Gulf Coast, where resources to support mindfulness in my professional practice and my personal practice are very limited. I've had to search to discover ways that I can grow in mindfulness. You may live in an area with similar limitations, or work and family commitments or lack of financial resources may stand in the way. So how do you begin incorporating mindfulness into your personal life?

A good place to start practicing mindfulness is with the breath. Try taking ten minutes during the day to sit quietly and notice your breathing. You can use the instructions for the mindful breathing practices in chapter 4. Try doing this every day for a week. Start a mindfulness journal and write about your experiences with the breathing practice. You can also take a mindfulness measure, explore your answers, and note areas that might need attention. Then focus on using your mindfulness practice to develop these areas.

Another thing you can do is make audio recordings of the body scan and sitting meditations in chapter 4. On different days, try mindfulness meditation, the lake meditation, the mountain meditation, and loving-kindness meditation.

You can also try the yoga poses described in chapter 5 or seek out another avenue to practicing yoga. Most community centers and gyms offer classes in yoga. In the past, when I came across people in my community who practiced yoga, I asked them where they went and which yoga instructors they'd recommend. A certain yoga center kept popping up as having excellent teachers, so I signed up for a ten-session yoga course. Participating in the course improved the yoga practice that I had started on my own years ago. Give yourself permission to take an hour every other day to practice yoga. Of course, cardiovascular exercise is also beneficial, and I've found that I can use it as a context for practicing mindfulness. I try to be mindful when I run, noticing my body move through space, my feet touching the ground, my breathing, and the sights, sounds, and smells around me.

If you feel like you need to take a more structured approach to incorporating mindfulness into your life, you can use the eight-week plan for chronic illness, pain, and stress outlined in chapter 9. This requires committing to practicing a formal mindfulness exercise, such as the body scan, sitting meditation, walking meditation, or yoga, for about an hour daily, most days of the week. As you open yourself to these practices, you'll find that certain exercises seem to work better for you. Let your experience guide you in developing a daily practice that emphasizes the exercises you find most useful.

An Example of Incorporating Mindfulness into Daily Life

I created a meditation space in my home where I can sit quietly and meditate every day. I usually spend at least thirty minutes in sitting meditation in the morning before I leave for work. I'm not an early morning person, so I wait for everyone else to leave for work and school before I take my seat. If you like to get up early, I hear it's a really nice experience to do so before the rest of the family is up. You don't need any special equipment, just a quiet place to sit. I did buy a *zafu* that I use for my sitting meditation. When the weather is nice, I take it outside to meditate. Inside, sometimes I sit in a large chair in which I can sit in a half-lotus position. I keep a stack of books nearby—some on mindfulness and some focused on inspirational readings. Sometimes I read a bit before I meditate. If I'm not feeling motivated to meditate, I may find something in my reading to bring to meditation that helps me get started.

Likewise, I've developed ways to incorporate informal mindfulness into daily life. I've found that eating my breakfast mindfully and in silence helps me remember to be kind to myself. I practice being mindful of my environment as I move through the day. I can't always do this on the weekend, when family members are around, but I usually can during the workweek. I also take ten-minute breathing breaks in the midmorning and afternoon, and a three-minute breathing space before I see each client. Another informal practice that I've found very helpful is using phone calls as a cue to wake up and attend to the present moment with mindfulness. I smile and notice my breathing as the phone rings for two or three rings. Then I pick up the phone. I also take a mindful moment before I make a phone call.

Incorporating mindfulness into your life doesn't have to cost a lot of money, but it will involve a time commitment. However, you'll find it well worth the time you spend practicing. Infusing your attention and awareness with the intention of being mindful, moment by moment, will change your life in unexpected and profound ways. You'll discover internal resources that will foster your well-being. You'll also grow in compassion and understanding of others and begin to feel more connected to the people in your life.

INCORPORATING MINDFULNESS INTO YOUR PROFESSIONAL OR WORK SETTINGS

When you begin incorporating mindfulness into your personal life, you'll naturally begin attending mindfully to your work environment as well, especially the people you work with on a daily basis. To further this natural progression, look around and notice how you might make some changes in your workday to encourage mindfulness. I work in an academic setting and have found a variety of ways to incorporate mindfulness into my professional life. For example, I started a weekly meeting to discuss research and plan studies exploring mindfulness, spirituality, and health psychology. Graduate students and colleagues interested in these areas are welcome to attend. I also now teach mindfulness exercises to my psychology graduate practicum students. I start each class with a formal mindfulness exercise led by either a student or myself. Together with some of my students, I conduct mindfulness-based groups for eating problems, anxiety, and stress, and we also offer a mindfulness-based weekend retreat for psychology graduate students and faculty. I've been invited to give presentations on mindfulness to a variety of audiences in my community. These opportunities to present on mindfulness have helped me discover other professionals in my community who are interested in mindfulness. They have become another source of support in developing mindfulness-based programs and also refer clients to my clinical practice.

Throughout the years, I've found colleagues in my community who practice mindfulness. We encourage each other and share ideas, books, and audio recordings that we've found helpful in our mindfulness practice. We keep each other up-to-date on new research studies on mindfulness that we come across. You might consider setting up a monthly meeting for yourself and other professionals to discuss and practice mindfulness together. See the resources section for suggested readings on mindfulness.

As you develop your own personal practice of mindfulness, you'll become aware of ways that you can introduce mindfulness into your professional life, wherever you may work, whether in a private practice, a hospital, a community mental health center, or a variety of other settings. A good place to begin is by incorporating mindfulness-based approaches with clients. I've found that guiding clients and others in mindfulness deepens my own experience and understanding of mindfulness.

I've learned a great deal from my clients, and asking clients for feedback on their experiences has been essential in improving my skills and awareness of what works and what doesn't.

Creating Awareness of Mindfulness

Depending on your work setting, you may be able to offer in-service presentations or workshops on mindfulness to coworkers. Or perhaps you can start a weekly meditation group for other therapists and others you work with. In any setting, you can take time each day to slow down and notice the people you work with. Become aware of moments of kindness, patience, and compassion that occur as you interact with others, and practice expressing gratitude to others who touch your life—not just your colleagues, but also the person who delivers the mail, maintenance workers, people who prepare your food, or those who answer the phone for you. Make eye contact with everyone you encounter on a daily basis and smile often!

You can begin a mindfulness e-mail group or Internet discussion group for people you work with to share experiences with mindfulness and other information, such as helpful readings or research on mindfulness. Another way to create awareness of mindfulness is to develop your own professional website where you can highlight mindfulness and include useful links for clients and others to learn more about mindfulness. If you already have a website, consider adding information about mindfulness to it.

Creating Spaces for Mindfulness

Create spaces in your work setting where people can sit quietly. You can start with your own office, adding a meditation space for you and your clients to practice in. See chapter 3 for recommendations on providing a good environment for mindfulness-based programs. If you can, it's highly worthwhile to find an outside space for people to practice walking meditation or to sit and appreciate the outdoor environment. Perhaps you have a small garden area or courtyard that could be made into a quiet area for you and others to practice mindfulness.

SUMMARY

You can practice mindfulness regardless of where you live or the resources available to you. I've provided examples of how you might incorporate mindfulness into your personal and professional life. As you develop your capacity to be mindful, you'll come to see that your personal and professional lives aren't really that separate. You'll begin experiencing the benefits of practicing mindfulness, and this may provide even more motivation to grow your mindfulness-based clinical practice—the topic of the next chapter.

chapter 11

Growing Your Mindfulness-Based Clinical Practice

Successful interventions are the best foundation on which to build and grow your practice. This is why evaluation is key. Therapists who want to treat their clients successfully must be able to evaluate the effectiveness of their mindfulness-based interventions. Using feedback from both process measures and client outcome evaluations, you can adapt or change interventions so that they're more effective. (*Process measures* evaluate what occurs within the session and the therapeutic relationship.) This chapter presents realistic methods for systematically assessing evidence-based protocols, and it explains how to develop effective evaluation procedures to help you grow your mindfulness-based clinical practice.

In this chapter, I'll also offer a few tips on growing your mindfulness-based practice, both for clinical populations and in other contexts. Researchers are reporting new and exciting programs for adapting mindfulness to a variety of nonclinical venues (Williams, 2006), including work environments, sports and exercise, and education. Many of these approaches focus on preventing illness or enhancing current functioning, rather than curing a problem.

DEVELOPING EVALUATION SYSTEMS

The growing research on evidence-based practice suggests several areas to be mindful of in creating effective interventions for clients. The American Psychological Association (2010) encourages therapists to periodically self-evaluate in at least four areas: best research evidence, patient characteristics, clinical expertise, and therapeutic actions. The following questions will help you consider how you're doing in these areas:

○ Are you aware of research that supports the clinical interventions you use with your clients?

○ When developing a treatment plan, do you consider client characteristics that can influence the effectiveness of the intervention, such as socioeconomic status, family and cultural issues, and readiness for change?

○ Do you have the clinical expertise to make appropriate decisions regarding desired outcomes, treatment options, and assessment of outcomes?

○ Do you evaluate how your clients are doing on a consistent basis, and respond to negative feedback to improve your practice?

You can create a more objective evaluation system for your mindfulness-based practice by developing a data collection plan. Over time, this will help you gather information on what's working and areas that need improvement in your mindfulness-based work with clients. Use the data you gather to make modifications to your approach and determine whether those changes are effective.

Data Collection Plan

As you reviewed the above questions, you might have noticed that in order to determine your clinical effectiveness with mindfulness-based treatments, you need to assess both process and outcome variables. Use the guidelines below to help you develop a system for evaluating the effectiveness of the care you provide your clients. You can then use the data you collect to provide information to clients and referral sources and to market your mindfulness-based programs.

BASELINE DATA

Create a spreadsheet in Microsoft Excel or similar data management software and begin keeping track of basic information about your clients. Include age, gender, diagnosis, and socioeconomic status. (You may already be using practice management software to record this information.)

Administer psychological tests to determine treatment goals, and then record client scores in the spreadsheet. As recommended in chapter 9, you can use the Outcome Rating Scale to establish a baseline, and at every session to track client progress. G. S. Brown and Takuya Minami (2010) note that a variety of outcome measures are available at no charge; they suggest consulting ACORN (A Collaborative Outcomes Resource Network; psychoutcomes.org) for more information. You can also administer more specific tests, such as the Symptom Checklist – 90 – Revised, the Minnesota Multiphasic Personality Inventory – 2, or the newer Minnesota Multiphasic Personality Inventory – 2 – Revised Form to assess a variety of clinical disorders and problems. Also include a measure of mindfulness. Enter all of these baseline scores in the spreadsheet.

TREATMENT DATA

At the beginning of every session, get feedback from clients on changes since the last session. I use the Outcome Rating Scale because it's quick to give and has good psychometric properties. You can use similar measures that you've found effective in your clinical work. You can even simply ask clients how they think their symptoms are on a scale from 0 (none) to 10 (very distressing) at the beginning of each session. Whatever measure you use, enter the score in your spreadsheet.

If you guide clients through a mindfulness exercise, you can administer the Toronto Mindfulness Scale, which assesses state mindfulness. And at the end of every session, get feedback on how the session went for the client. I use the Session Rating Scale, described in chapter 7, as a process measure to reflect the status of my therapeutic relationship with clients. Enter all scores in your spreadsheet.

END-OF-TREATMENT DATA AND FOLLOW-UP SESSION

At the last session, administer the same psychological tests and outcome, process, and mindfulness measures that you gave at the first session and during treatment. Include all of these scores in your spreadsheet. Administer these same tests again at follow-up sessions, typically at one, three and six months, and at one year. This is important in determining whether clients are maintaining treatment gains. If they aren't, you might suggest that they return for a booster session.

Making Sense of Outcome and Process Data

Within a few months of recording the data outlined above, you'll have enough information to begin evaluating how your clients are doing. You can use simple summary data such as the means of clients' scores to determine how many of your clients are improving, getting worse, or not changing much. If the data indicates your clients are improving, hooray! If scores generally aren't changing or are getting worse, you need to review your work and look for ways to improve your effectiveness. You might need to consult with colleagues to determine whether you're implementing an intervention correctly, or you may need a refresher course on a particular topic to improve your expertise.

By reviewing the data for clients with different types of problems and goals and noting which responded better to your mindfulness-based interventions, you might begin seeing patterns of what works best for certain types of clients, problems, and goals. Research shows that therapists who consistently demonstrate good client outcomes also continually strive to evaluate their performance and improve their clinical skills and the therapeutic alliance, resulting in higher-quality care (Duncan, Miller, Wampold, & Hubble, 2010; American Psychological Association, 2010).

Scott Miller (2009) presented data from several research studies supporting the idea that some therapists produce significantly better client outcomes than others and refers to these therapists as "supershrinks," a term first proffered in 1974 by D. F. Ricks to describe a group of therapists who had excellent client outcomes. According to Miller (2009), the clients of "supershrinks" are more likely to stay in therapy and improve compared to other therapists. His research shows that these highly effective therapists are alert to how engaged their clients are in the therapeutic experience, and that they seek to improve client engagement by getting feedback from clients and being open to what they learn. Developing your own mindfulness practice may foster your ability to accept feedback from clients. Then, by reflecting on the feedback and data you collect and checking in with clients at each session, you can improve their engagement in the therapeutic experience and improve the overall effectiveness of your interventions.

You can also use your data to compare your effectiveness to that of other therapists, which can provide additional information on how you might improve your approach. For example, you might find that only 40 percent of your clients find breathing meditation to be helpful, compared to research showing that 60 percent of clients typically find it helpful. In response to this discrepancy, you might choose to review the instructions you use with your clients and also take a refresher class on breathing meditation. You could also ask clients for feedback on your presentation of the exercise: What helps and what doesn't help? Their responses might help you discover better ways to introduce breathing meditation. For example, clients may report that your tone of voice is distracting and makes it difficult to attend to their breathing. In this case, you could practice changing the tone of your voice to see if this helps clients better focus on their breathing while doing this exercise.

STRATEGIES FOR GROWING YOUR MINDFULNESS-BASED PRACTICE

You may be satisfied with the amount of clinical work you do and therefore aren't interested in growing your practice. But if you are interested in expanding your practice, the information you gather on the effectiveness of your interventions can be useful. While it's beyond the scope of this book to provide a marketing plan for your practice, there are many strategies for increasing your mindfulness-based practice, and I'll present four that you can use to get started: collaborating with other professionals, providing mindfulness-based interventions for specific populations, offering presentations on mindfulness in the community at large, and cultivating referral sources. These strategies flow easily from using an evidence-based approach to integrate mindfulness into your clinical practice. (For more detailed and comprehensive information on marketing your clinical practice, consult your professional organizations.)

In chapter 10, I discussed ways you might integrate mindfulness into your professional life. I suggested collaborating with other professionals when developing mindfulness-based programs in order to improve your effectiveness and also to create awareness about mindfulness in your local community. Offer to speak to local professional organizations on mindfulness. Provide suggestions or guidelines for when their patients might benefit from a mindfulness-based intervention. As mentioned in chapter 10, you could also start a local group for professionals who are interested in practicing mindfulness and learning more about it. Collaborating with other professionals is also an important strategy in developing referral sources, discussed below.

A second strategy is to focus on providing mindfulness-based groups or individual therapy for particular populations. For example, some clinicians provide mindfulness-based interventions to geriatric clients, while others offer programs for eating disorders. You can advertise mindfulness-based specialty programs and market to people or places that are more likely to refer particular populations or problems to you. For example, if you offer mindfulness-based groups for geriatric populations, you can market to nursing homes, caregivers of the elderly, and health care professionals who specialize in geriatrics.

Another approach to growing your mindfulness practice is to contact community centers, health care centers, schools, and churches and offer to do an informational presentation or a brief workshop on mindfulness. In many communities, the average citizen isn't familiar with the concept of mindfulness, so it's likely that anytime you educate people about mindfulness, you'll create potential referrals.

Finally, you can provide the data you collect on your clinical effectiveness to a variety of potential referral sources. Give your current clients information on your effectiveness in helping people change using mindfulness-based interventions. Clients who improve and are aware of your success are more likely to refer family, friends, and colleagues to you. These referrals may be more effective if clients can provide written documentation of your effectiveness. You can also send this data to health care professionals and third-party payers such as insurance companies to provide objective evidence about the effectiveness of the work you do. These potential referral sources are likely to be impressed with this information and therefore more confident about referring clients to you.

FUTURE DIRECTIONS FOR MINDFULNESS-BASED PRACTICE

Most of the mindfulness-based programs reported thus far have focused on helping people with significant clinical problems. Reports on new directions for mindfulness-based practice suggest that mindfulness-based interventions can also be helpful in enhancing health and preventing illness (Williams, 2006). In the last few years, researchers have started evaluating mindfulness-based interventions in the workplace, for improving sports performance and exercise effectiveness, and in schools. In most cases, participants in these programs don't have significant or clinical levels of psychological distress. They simply want to improve or enhance their health or their performance in various activities.

All three venues (the workplace, sports, and school settings) are avenues you might explore in growing your practice. However, don't feel limited to these settings. I recently heard a story about a police department that was offering a mindfulness-based program for police officers to help them cope with work stress and reduce negative job-related consequences, such as burnout and chronic anger. Mindfulness can help people improve their ability to cope with stress and enhance their functioning in a variety of settings. Be open to the possibilities in your community.

Mindfulness-Based Approaches in the Workplace

Mindfulness-based stress reduction can help improve health and engender wellness. Kimberly Williams (2006) reports on MBSR as an option that can be offered through worksite wellness programs. She notes that the rising cost of health care for employees has become a challenge for many businesses. Because MBSR targets many of the important risk factors in the major causes of illness and death and is effective in reducing stress and helping people with a variety of problems, it can help prevent illness and burnout and therefore is a cost-efficient approach. Interventions that help prevent severe or chronic diseases are less costly to implement than treatment of such diseases.

Williams (2006) notes that while many company-based employee assistance programs provide good health assessments, screening, and psychoeducational programs, several research reviews have indicated that these services don't lead to long-term changes because they don't provide employees with skills to help them change health risk behaviors. MBSR teaches skills that help people self-regulate more effectively and take responsibility for their health care. Although there are only a few research reports on the effectiveness of MBSR in the workplace, the popular press has begun to promote mindfulness as an important new concept for businesses to integrate into the work environment. You might find that businesses in your community are open to the idea of having you providing MBSR in the workplace or are interested in referring employees to your practice.

Mindfulness-Based Approaches in Sports

A few studies suggest that mindfulness-based approaches might help athletes improve their performance or help coaches be more effective. Patricia Collard and James Walsh (2008) report on training coaches in mindfulness to help them develop a better balance between work and other aspects of life. They incorporate the body scan, breathing exercises, yoga, and sitting meditation into their program and recommend that the coaches do at least one formal meditation every day. The data they've collected suggests that as a result of the program, coaches felt they were less stressed and calmer, and tended to be in a better mood. Collard and Walsh didn't provide data on whether participants' coaching effectiveness improved; however, most of the coaches said that they wanted to continue to attend weekly sessions on mindfulness.

In an article published in 2004, Frank Gardner and Zella Moore explored using a mindfulness-based approach to improve athletic performance. Most other sport psychology approaches use cognitive techniques to help athletes mentally counter negative thoughts and feelings or to distract themselves from these negative experiences. Gardner and Moore found that helping athletes develop a nonjudgmental present-moment awareness of their internal experiences improved athletic performance as compared to using cognitive strategies to control internal experiences.

As discussed in previous chapters, mindfulness fosters awareness and acceptance of all internal experiences—negative and positive. This helps athletes understand the temporary nature of these negative experiences and learn to let go of them. In their program, Gardner and Moore taught both general mindfulness exercises, such as breathing awareness and the body scan, and sport-specific practices, such as mindful pregame stretching and mindful drills or practice exercises. Athletes used these techniques at home and during practice and competition. If you do sport psychology work in your practice, you might consider exploring how you can integrate mindfulness-based techniques into sports and exercise programs.

Mindfulness-Based Approaches in Schools

School administrators are becoming interested in the positive effects of mindfulness on schoolchildren and teachers. Several studies that have looked at mindfulness-based school interventions for nonclinical students suggest that these programs can improve students' attention, social skills, and academic performance (Burke, 2010). Researchers have also started to evaluate how mindfulness training can help teachers' emotional balance (Shapiro & Carlson, 2009). An example is the Cultivating Emotional Balance project, started in San Francisco in 2002 for training secondary school teachers in mindfulness (Shapiro & Carlson, 2009). In this program, teachers learn meditation, awareness in everyday life, and skills to enhance their emotional intelligence.

This opens the door to another avenue that you might explore in your community: offering mindfulness-based interventions for enhancing the overall psychosocial functioning of teachers or students, either in school settings or in your office. Even students and teachers who don't have significant clinical problems can benefit from developing a mindfulness practice.

SCIENCE, PRACTICE, AND WAKING UP TO LIFE

I hope I've encouraged you to embrace both the science and the practice of mindfulness in helping people change. Mindfulness fosters openness to whatever exists or occurs in the present moment and also enhances the ability to observe internal and external experiences nonjudgmentally. Through your own personal practice, you can put these qualities to work in developing, improving, and growing your practice. An evidence-based perspective requires objective observation of what works and what doesn't, yet clinicians rarely get feedback on how well their clients are responding to the interventions they conduct. Enhancing your own mindfulness will help you accept negative feedback from your clients and use this information to improve client outcomes.

A personal mindfulness practice will improve your own emotional functioning and ground you in an adaptive moment-by-moment experience of your personal and professional life. Through your practice, you'll discover that the personal and the professional really aren't separate; your professional and personal experiences influence each other and, ultimately, your effectiveness with clients.

Wake up to life! Don't lose one second asleep to the present moment. Attend to yourself, your clients, and all you encounter with loving-kindness, patience, and openness. You will suffer at times, but I guarantee that your life will be richer and that you'll learn to appreciate all things and all experiences.

Resources

Here are some suggested readings and audio recordings to help you learn more about mindfulness. Some of these resources include inspirational writings or poetry that you can use to introduce your clients to the concept of mindfulness or help them explore it and deepen their practice.

READINGS

Brantley, J. (2007). *Calming your anxious mind* (3rd ed.). Oakland, CA: New Harbinger Publications.

Herrigel, E. (1960). *The method of Zen.* New York: Vintage Books.

Kabat-Zinn, J. (1990). *Full catastrophe living: Using the wisdom of your body and mind to face stress, pain, and illness.* New York: Bantam Dell.

Kabat-Zinn, J. (1994). *Wherever you go, there you are: Mindfulness meditation in everyday life.* New York: Hyperion.

Kornfield, J. (1993). *A path with heart: A guide through the perils and promises of spiritual life.* New York: Bantam.

Kumar, S. M. (2005). *Grieving mindfully: A compassionate and spiritual guide to coping with loss.* Oakland, CA: New Harbinger Publications.

McQuaid, J. R., & Carmona, P. E. (2004). *Peaceful mind: Using meditation and cognitive behavioral psychology to overcome depression,* Oakland, CA: New Harbinger Publications.

Nhat Hanh, T. (1993). *The blooming of a lotus: Guided meditation for achieving the miracle of mindfulness.* Boston, MA: Beacon Press.

Roshi, T. M. (2001). *Appreciate your life: The essence of Zen practice.* Boston, MA: Shambhala Publications.

Suzuki, D. T. (1960). *Manual of Zen Buddhism.* New York: Grove Press.

Thoreau, H. D. (2001). *Henry David Thoreau: Collected essays and poems* (E. H. Witherell, Ed.). New York: Literary Classics of the United States.

YOGA

Carroll, C., & Kimata, L. (2000). *Partner yoga: Making contact for physical, emotional, and spiritual growth.* New York: Rodale Books.

Edmond, M. (2004). *The joy of partner yoga.* New York: Sterling Publishing.

Kurland, Z. (2007). *Morning yoga workouts.* Champagne, IL: Human Kinetics.

AUDIO RECORDINGS

Kabat-Zinn, J. (2005). *Coming to our senses: Healing ourselves and the world through mindfulness.* New York: Hyperion.

Kabat-Zinn, J. (2006). *Mindfulness for beginners: Exploring the infinite potential that lies within this very moment.* Audio recording. Louisville, CO: Sounds True.

Kornfield, J. (2010). *Guided meditation: Six essential practices to cultivate love, awareness, and wisdom.* Audio recording. Louisville, CO: Sounds True.

Nhat Hanh, T. (2000). *Mindful living collectors edition: A collection of teachings on love, mindfulness, and meditation.* Audio recording. 5-CD set. Louisville, CO: Sounds True.

References

American Psychological Association. (2010). EBPP Checklist for Psychologists. *Good Practice*, Fall 2009/Winter 2010. Washington, DC: American Psychological Practice Association.

Arch, J. J., & Craske, M. G. (2006). Mechanisms of mindfulness: Emotion regulation following a focused breathing induction. *Behavior Research and Therapy, 44*, 1849-1858.

Baer, R. A. (Ed.). (2006). *Mindfulness-based treatment approaches: Clinician's guide to evidence base and applications.* Burlington, MA: Academic Press.

Baer, R. A., Smith, G. T., & Allen, K. B. (2004). Assessment of mindfulness by self-report: The Kentucky Inventory of Mindfulness Skills. *Assessment, 11*, 191-206.

Baer, R. A., Smith, G., Hopkins, J., Krietemeyer, J., & Toney, L. (2006). Using self-report assessment methods to explore facets of mindfulness. *Assessment, 13*, 27-45.

Baer, R. A., Walsh, E., & Lykins, E. L. B. (2009). Assessment of mindfulness. In F. Didonna (Ed.), *Clinical handbook of mindfulness.* New York: Springer.

Barnes, S., Brown, K. W., Krusemarck, E., Campbell, W. K., & Rogge, R. D. (2007). The role of mindfulness in romantic relationship satisfaction and responses to relationship stress. *Journal of Marital and Family Therapy, 33*, 482-500.

Barnhofer, T., & Crane, C. (2006). Mindfulness-based cognitive therapy for depression and suicidality. In R. A. Baer (Ed.), *Mindfulness-based treatment approaches: Clinician's guide to evidence base and applications.* Burlington, MA: Academic Press.

Beck, A. T., Steer, R. A., & Brown, G. K. (1996). *BDI-II Manual.* San Antonio, TX: Psych Corp.

Ben-Porath, Y. S., & Tellegen, A. (2007). *MMPI-2-RF (Minnesota Multiphasic Personality Inventory – 2 – Revised Form).* San Antonio, TX: PsychCorp.

Biegel, G. M., Brown, K. W., Shapiro, S. L., & Schubert, C. M. (2009). Mindfulness-based stress reduction for the treatment of adolescent psychiatric outpatients: A randomized clinical trial. *Journal of Consulting and Clinical Psychology, 77,* 855-866.

Bishop, S. R., Lau, M., Shapiro, S., Carlson, L., Anderson, N. D., Carmody, J., et al. (2004). Mindfulness: A proposed operational definition. *Clinical Psychology: Science and Practice, 11,* 230-241.

Brown, G. S., & Minami, T. (2010). Outcomes management, reimbursement, and the future of psychotherapy. In B. L. Duncan, S. D. Miller, B. E. Wampold, & M. A. Hubble (Eds.), *The heart and soul of change: Delivering what works in therapy* (2nd ed.). Washington, DC: American Psychological Association.

Brown, K. W., & Cordon, S. (2009). Toward a phenomenology of mindfulness: Subjective experience and emotional correlates. In F. Didonna (Ed.), *Clinical handbook of mindfulness.* New York: Springer.

Brown, K. W., & Ryan, R. (2003). The benefits of being present: Mindfulness and its role in psychological well-being. *Journal of Personality and Social Psychology, 84,* 822-848.

Brown, K. W., & Ryan, R. (2004). Perils and promise in defining and measuring mindfulness: Observations from experience. *Clinical Psychology: Science and Practice, 11,* 242-248.

Brown, K. W., Ryan, R., & Creswell, J. D. (2007a). Mindfulness: Theoretical foundations and evidence for its salutary effects. *Psychological Inquiry, 18,* 211-237.

Brown, K. W., Ryan, R., & Creswell, J. D. (2007b). Addressing fundamental questions about mindfulness. *Psychological Inquiry, 18,* 272-281.

Bucheld, N., Grossman, P., & Walach, H. (2001). Measuring mindfulness in insight meditation (vipassana) and meditation-based psychotherapy: The development of the Freiburg Mindfulness Inventory (FMI). *Journal for Meditation and Meditation Research, 1,* 11-34.

Burke, C. A. (2010). Mindfulness-based approaches with children and adolescents: A preliminary review of current research in an emergent field. *Journal of Child and Family Studies, 19,* 133-144.

Butcher, J. N., Dahlstrom, W. G., Graham, J. R., Tellegen, A., & Kaemmer, B. (1989). *Manual for the Minnesota Multiphasic Personality Inventory – 2: MMPI-2. Manual for administration and scoring.* Minneapolis, MN: University of Minnesota Press.

Carlson, L., & Brown, K. (2005). Validation of the Mindful Attention Awareness Scale in a cancer population. *Journal of Psychosomatic Research, 58,* 29-33.

Carson, J. W., Carson, K. M., Gil, K. M., & Baucom, D. H. (2006). Mindfulness-based relationship enhancement (MBRE) in couples. In R. A. Baer (Ed.), *Mindfulness-based treatment approaches: Clinician's guide to evidence base and applications.* Burlington, MA: Academic Press.

Chadwick, P., Hember, M., Symes, J., Peters, E., Kuipers, E., & Dagnan, D. (2008). Responding mindfully to unpleasant thoughts and images: Reliability and validity of the Southampton Mindfulness Questionnaire (SMQ). *British Journal of Clinical Psychology, 47*, 451-455.

Chatzisarantis, N., & Hagger, M. (2007). Mindfulness and the intention-behavior relationship within the theory of planned behavior. *Personality and Social Psychology Bulletin, 33*, 663-676.

Christopher, J. C., Christopher, S. E., Dunnagan, T., & Schure, M. (2006). Teaching self-care through mindfulness practices: The application of yoga, meditation, and qigong to counselor training. *Journal of Humanistic Psychology, 46*, 495-509.

Clendenin, D. B. (2002, November 25). Thanksgiving 2002: Giving thanks in an age of enlightenment. Retrieved April 30, 2010, from www.journeywithjesus.net/Essays/20021125JJ.shtml.

Coffey, K., & Hartman, M. (2008). Mechanisms of action in the inverse relationship between mindfulness and psychological distress. *Complementary Health and Practice Review, 13*, 79-91.

Coffman, S. J., Dimidjian, S., & Baer, R. A. (2006). Mindfulness-based cognitive therapy for prevention of depressive relapse. In R. A. Baer (Ed.), *Mindfulness-based treatment approaches: Clinician's guide to evidence base and applications*. Burlington, MA: Academic Press.

Collard, P., & Walsh, J. (2008). Sensory awareness mindfulness training in coaching: Accepting life's challenges. *Journal of Rational-Emotive and Cognitive-Behavior Therapy, 26*, 30-37.

Conners, C. K., & MHS Staff. (2000). *Conners' Continuous Performance Test (CPT II): Computer program for Windows technical guide and software manual*. North Tonawanda, NY: Multi-Health Systems.

Costa, P. T., Jr., & McCrae, R. R. (1992). *NEO PI-R: Professional manual*. Odessa, FL: Psychological Assessment Resources.

Creswell, J. D., Way, B. M., Eisenberger, N. I., & Lieberman, M. D. (2007). Neural correlates of dispositional mindfulness during affect labeling. *Psychosomatic Medicine, 69*, 560-565.

Cropley, M., Ussher, M., & Charitou, E. (2007). Acute effects of a guided relaxation routine (body scan) on tobacco withdrawal symptoms and cravings in abstinent smokers. *Addiction, 102*, 989-993.

Dahl, J., & Lundgren, T. (2006). Acceptance and commitment therapy (ACT) in the treatment of chronic pain. In R. A. Baer (Ed.), *Mindfulness-based treatment approaches: Clinician's guide to evidence base and applications*. Burlington, MA: Academic Press.

Davidson, R., Kabat-Zinn, J., Schumacher, J., Rosenkranz, M., Muller, D., Santorelli, S., et al. (2003). Alterations in brain and immune function produced by mindfulness meditation. *Psychosomatic Medicine, 65*, 564-570.

Derogatis, L. R. (1992). *SCL-90-R: Administration, Scoring & Procedures Manual II*. Towson, MD: Clinical Psychometric Research.

Desikachar, T. K. V. (1999). *The heart of yoga: Developing a personal practice.* Rochester, VT: Inner Traditions International.

Didonna, F. (2009). Introduction: Where new and old paths to dealing with suffering meet. In F. Didonna (Ed.), *Clinical handbook of mindfulness.* New York: Springer.

Ditto, B., Eclache, M., & Goldman, N. (2006). Short-term autonomic and cardiovascular effects of mindfulness body scan meditation. *Annals of Behavioral Medicine, 32,* 227-234.

Duncan, B., Miller, S. D., Reynolds, L., Sparks, J., Claud, D., & Brown, J. (2004). The Session Rating Scale: Psychometric properties of a "working" alliance scale. *Journal of Brief Therapy* 3(1):3-12.

Duncan, B. L., Miller, S. D., Wampold, B. E., & Hubble, M. A. (Eds.). (2010). *The heart and soul of change: Delivering what works in therapy* (2nd ed.). Washington, DC: American Psychological Association.

Feldman, G., Hayes, A., Kumar, S., Greeson, J., & Laurenceau, J. (2007). Mindfulness and emotion regulation: The development and initial validation of the Cognitive and Affective Mindfulness Scale – Revised (CMS-R). *Journal of Psychopathology and Behavioral Assessment, 29,* 177-190.

Gage, W. H., Sleik, R. J., Polych, M. A., McKenzie, N. C., & Brown, L. A. (2003). The allocation of attention during locomotion is altered by anxiety. *Experimental Brain Research, 150,* 385-394.

Gardner, D. M. (2004). *Eating Disorder Inventory – 3.* Lutz, FL: Psychological Assessment Resources.

Gardner, F. L., & Moore, Z. E. (2004). A mindfulness-acceptance-commitment-based approach to athletic performance enhancement: Theoretical considerations. *Behavior Therapy, 35,* 707-723.

Greeson, J. M., Rosenzweig, S., Vogel, W. H., Greener, M., Perry, A., & Brainard, G. C. (2001). Mindfulness meditation and stress physiology in medical students (abstract). *Psychosomatic Medicine, 63,* 158.

Grepmair, L., Mitterlehner, F., Loew, T., Bachler, E., Rother, W., & Nickel, M. (2007). Promoting mindfulness in psychotherapists in training influences the treatment results of their patients: A randomized, double-blind, controlled study. *Psychotherapy and Psychosomatics, 76,* 332-338.

Grepmair, L., Mitterlehner, F., Loew, T., & Nickel, M. (2007). Promotion of mindfulness in psycho-therapists in training: Preliminary study. *European Psychiatry, 22,* 485-489.

Grossman, P. (2008). On measuring mindfulness in psychosomatic and psychological research. *Journal of Psychosomatic Research, 64,* 405-408.

Grossman, P., Niemann, L., Schmidt, S., & Walach, H. (2004). Mindfulness-based stress reduction and health benefits: A meta-analysis. *Journal of Psychosomatic Research, 5,* 35-43.

Herndon, F. (2008). Testing mindfulness with perceptual and cognitive factors: External vs. internal encoding, and the Cognitive Failures Questionnaire. *Personality and Individual Differences, 44,* 32-41.

Holmes, T. H., and Rahe, R. H. (1967). The Social Readjustment Rating Scale. *Journal of Psychosomatic Research 11*, 213-218.

Hubble, M. A., Duncan, B. L., & Miller, S. D. (1999). *The heart and soul of change: What works in therapy.* Washington, DC: American Psychological Association.

Hubble, M. A., Duncan, B. L., Miller, S. D., & Wampold, B. E. (2010). Introduction. In B. L. Duncan, S. D. Miller, B. E. Wampold, & M. A. Hubble (Eds.), *The heart and soul of change: Delivering what works in therapy* (2nd ed.). Washington, DC: American Psychological Association.

Jain, S., Shapiro, S. L., Swanick, S., Roesch, S. C., Mills, P. J., Bell, I., et al. (2007). A randomized controlled trial of mindfulness meditation versus relaxation training: Effects on distress, positive states of mind, rumination, and distraction. *Annals of Behavioral Medicine, 33*, 11-21.

Jha, A. P., Krompinger, J., & Baime, J. J. (2007). Mindfulness training modifies subsystems of attention. *Cognitive, Affective, and Behavioral Neuroscience, 7*, 109-119.

Kabat-Zinn, J. (1990). *Full catastrophe living: Using the wisdom of your body and mind to face stress, pain, and illness.* New York: Bantam Dell.

Kabat-Zinn, J. (1994). *Wherever you go, there you are: Mindfulness meditation in everyday life.* New York: Hyperion.

Kabat-Zinn, J. (2005). *Coming to our senses: Healing ourselves and the world through mindfulness.* New York: Hyperion.

Kabat-Zinn, J. (2006). *Mindfulness for beginners: Exploring the infinite potential that lies within this very moment.* Audio recording. Louisville, CO: Sounds True.

Kornfield, J. (1993). *A path with heart: A guide through the perils and promises of spiritual life.* New York: Bantam Books.

Kristeller, J. L., Baer, R. A., & Quillian-Wolever, R. (2006). Mindfulness-based approaches to eating disorders. In R. A. Baer (Ed.), *Mindfulness-based treatment approaches: Clinician's guide to evidence base and applications.* Burlington, MA: Academic Press.

Labbé, E. (1999). Management of headache, other than migraine. In J. Stockman & J. Lohr (Eds.), *Essence of pediatrics.* New York: W. B. Saunders.

Labbé, E. (2009). *Mindfulness training: Evaluating spirituality, personality, and health outcome.* Paper presented at the annual meeting of the Southeastern Psychological Association, New Orleans, LA.

Labbé, E., & Fobes, A. (2010). Evaluating the interplay between spirituality, personality, and stress. *Applied Psychophysiology and Biofeedback, 35*, 141-146.

Lau, M., Bishop, S., Segal, Z., Buis, T., Anderson, N., Carlson, L., et al. (2006). The Toronto Mindfulness Scale: Development and validation. *Journal of Clinical Psychology, 62*, 1445-1467.

Lazar, S. W., Kerr, C., Wasserman, R., Gray, J. R., Greve, D. N., Treadway, M. T., et al. (2005). Meditation experience is associated with increased cortical thickness. *Neuroreport, 16,* 1893-1897.

Linehan, M. (1993). *Cognitive-behavioral treatment of borderline personality disorder.* New York: Guilford.

Ludwig, D. S., & Kabat-Zinn, J. (2008). Mindfulness in medicine. *Journal of the American Medical Association, 300,* 1350-1352.

Lutz, A., Brefczynski-Lewis, J., Johnstone, T., & Davidson, R. J. (2008). Regulation of the neural circuitry of emotion by compassion meditation: Effects of meditative expertise. *Plos One, 3,* e1897.

Lutz, A., Greischar, L. L., Perlman, D. M., & Davidson, R. J. (2009). BOLD signal in insula is differentially related to cardiac function during compassion meditation in experts vs. novices. *NeuroImage, 47,* 1038-1046.

Lutz, A., Greischar, L. L., Rawlings, N. B., Ricard, M., & Davidson, R. J. (2004). Long-term meditators self-induce high-amplitude gamma synchrony during mental practice. *Proceedings of the National Academy of Sciences, 101,* 16369-16373.

McBee, L. (2009). Mindfulness-based elder care: Communicating mindfulness to frail elders and their caregivers. In F. Didonna (Ed.), *Clinical handbook of mindfulness.* New York: Springer.

Melzack, R. (1975). The McGill Pain Questionnaire: Major properties and scoring methods. *Pain 1,* 277-299.

Miller, S. D. (2009). *Supershrinks: Learning from the field's most effective practitioners.* Annual Mobile Association of Psychologists Continuing Education, Biloxi, MS.

Miller, S. D., Duncan, B. L., Brown, J., Sparks, J. A., & Claud, D. (2003). The Outcome Rating Scale: A preliminary study of the reliability, validity, and feasibility of a brief visual analog measure. *Journal of Brief Therapy* 2(2):91-100.

Nhat Hanh, T. (1993). *The blooming of a lotus: Guided meditation for achieving the miracle of mindfulness.* Boston, MA: Beacon Press.

Nhat Hanh, T. (2000). *Mindful living collectors edition: A collection of teachings on love, mindfulness, and meditation.* Audio recording. 5-CD set. Louisville, CO: Sounds True.

Ospina, M. B., Bond, K., Karkhaneh, M., Buscemi, N., Dryden, D. M., Barnes, V., et al. (2008). Clinical trials of meditation practices in health care: Characteristics and quality. *Journal of Alternative and Complementary Medicine, 14,* 1199-1213.

Rathus, J. H., Cavuoto, N., & Passarelli, V. (2006). Dialectical behavior therapy (DBT): A mindfulness-based treatment for intimate partner violence. In R. A. Baer (Ed.), *Mindfulness-based treatment approaches: Clinician's guide to evidence base and applications.* Burlington, MA: Academic Press.

Raz, A., & Buhle, J. (2006). Typologies of attentional networks. *Nature Reviews. Neuroscience, 7*, 367-379.

Rejeski, W. J. (2008). Mindfulness: Reconnecting the body and mind in geriatric medicine and gerontology. *Gerontologist, 48*, 135-141.

Ricks, D. F. (1974). Supershrink: Methods of a therapist judged successful on the basis of adult outcomes of adolescent patients. In D. F. Ricks, M. Roff, & A. Thomas (Eds.), *Life history research in psychopathology*, vol. 3. Minneapolis: University of Minnesota Press.

Robertson, I. H., & Garavan, H. (2004). Vigilant attention. In M. S. Gazzaniga (Ed.), *The cognitive neurosciences*. New York: MIT Press.

Roemer, L., Orsillo, S. M., & Salters-Pedneault, K. (2008). Efficacy of an acceptance-based behavior therapy for generalized anxiety disorder: Evaluation in a randomized controlled trial. *Journal of Consulting and Clinical Psychology, 76*, 1083-1089.

Roemer, L., Salters-Pedneault, K., & Orsillo, S. M. (2006). Incorporating mindfulness- and acceptance-based strategies in the treatment of generalized anxiety disorder. In R. A. Baer (Ed.), *Mindfulness-based treatment approaches: Clinician's guide to evidence base and applications*. Burlington, MA: Academic Press.

Salmon, P., Lush, E., Jablonski, M., & Sephton, S. E. (2009). Yoga and mindfulness: Clinical aspects of an ancient mind/body practice. *Cognitive and Behavioral Practice, 16*, 59-72.

Schure, M. B., Christopher, J., & Christopher, S. (2008). Mind-body medicine and the art of self-care: Teaching mindfulness to counseling students through yoga, meditation, and qigong. *Journal of Counseling and Development, 86*, 47-56.

Schwartz, G. E. (1984). Psychobiology of health: A new synthesis. In B. L. Hammonds & C. J. Scheirer (Eds.), *Psychology and health: Master lecture series*, vol. 3. Washington, DC: American Psychological Association.

Schwartz, G. E. (1990). Psychobiology of repression and health: A systems approach. In J. Singer (Ed.), *Repression and dissociation: Implications for personality theory, psychopathology, and health*. Chicago: University of Chicago Press.

Shapiro, S. L., Brown, K. W., & Biegel, G. M. (2007). Teaching self-care to caregivers: Effects of mindfulness-based stress reduction on the mental health of therapists in training. *Training and Education in Professional Psychology, 1*, 105-115.

Shapiro, S. L., Brown, K. W., & Bittlingmayer, H. (2009, March). *The moderation of mindfulness-based reduction effects by trait mindfulness: A randomized controlled trial*. Poster presented at the 7th Annual International Scientific Conference for Clinicians, Researchers, and Educators, Worcester, MA.

Shapiro, S. L., & Carlson, L. E. (2009). *The art and science of mindfulness: Integrating mindfulness into psychology and the helping professions.* Washington, DC: American Psychological Association.

Shapiro, S. L., & Schwartz, G. E. (2000). The role of intention in self-regulation: Toward intentional systemic mindfulness. In M. Boekaerts, P. R. Pintrich, & M. Zeidner (Eds.), *Handbook of Self-Regulation.* San Diego, CA: Academic Press.

Siegel, R. D., Germer, C. K., & Olendzki, A. (2009). Mindfulness: What is it? Where did it come from? In F. Didonna (Ed.), *Clinical handbook of mindfulness.* New York: Springer.

Smith, A. (2006). "Like waking up from a dream": Mindfulness training for older people with anxiety and depression. In R. A. Baer (Ed.), *Mindfulness-based treatment approaches: Clinician's guide to evidence base and applications.* Burlington, MA: Academic Press.

Spielberger, C. D., Gorsuch, R. L., & Lushene, R. (1970). *Manual for the State-Trait Anxiety Inventory: STAI ("Self-Evaluation Questionnaire").* Palo Alto, CA: Consulting Psychologists Press.

Stanley, S., Reitzel, L. R., Wingate, L. R., Cukrowicz, K. C., Lima, E. N., & Joiner, T. E. (2006). Mindfulness: A primrose path for therapists using manualized treatments? *Journal of Cognitive Psychotherapy: An International Quarterly, 20,* 327-335.

Sue, D., & Sue, D. M. (2008). *Foundations of counseling and psychotherapy: Evidence-based practices for a diverse society.* Hoboken, NJ: Wiley.

Tangney, J. P., Baumeister, R. F., & Boone, A. L. (2004). High self-control predicts good adjustment, less pathology, better grades, and interpersonal success. *Journal of Personality, 72,* 271-322.

Taylor, S. E. (2008). *Health psychology* (7th ed.). New York: McGraw-Hill.

Thompson, M., & Gauntlett-Gilbert, J. (2008). Mindfulness with children and adolescents: Effective clinical application. *Clinical Child Psychology and Psychiatry, 13,* 395-407.

Treadway, M. T., & Lazar, S. W. (2009). The neurobiology of mindfulness. In F. Didonna (Ed.), *Clinical handbook of mindfulness.* New York: Springer.

Walach, H., Buchheld, N., Buttenmüller, V., Kleinknecht, N., & Schmidt, S. (2006). Measuring mindfulness: The Freiburg Mindfulness Inventory (FMI). *Personality and Individual Differences, 40,* 1543-1555.

Walsh, R., & Shapiro, S. L. (2006). The meeting of meditative disciplines and Western psychology: A mutually enriching dialogue. *American Psychologist, 61,* 227-239.

Welch, S. S., Rizvi, S., & Dimidjian, S. (2006). Mindfulness in dialectical behavior therapy for borderline personality disorder. In R. A. Baer (Ed.), *Mindfulness-based treatment approaches: Clinician's guide to evidence base and applications.* Burlington, MA: Academic Press.

Weiner, N. (1948). *Cybernetics: Control and communication in the animal and the machine.* New York: Wiley.

West, A. M., & Loverich, T. M. (2009, March). *Measuring mindfulness in adolescence: An exploration of four mindfulness measures in an adolescent sample.* Paper presented at the 7th Annual International Scientific Conference for Clinicians, Researchers, and Educators, Worcester, MA. Williams, K. (2006). Mindfulness-based stress reduction (MBSR) in a worksite wellness program. In R. A. Baer (Ed.), *Mindfulness-based treatment approaches: Clinician's guide to evidence base and applications.* Burlington, MA: Academic Press.

Wolever, R. Q., & Best, J. L. (2009). Mindfulness-based approaches to eating disorders. In F. Didonna (Ed.), *Clinical handbook of mindfulness.* New York: Springer.

Zylowska, L., Smalley, S. L., & Schwartz, J. M. (2009). Mindfulness awareness and ADHD. In F. Didonna (Ed.), *Clinical handbook of mindfulness.* New York: Springer.

Elise E. Labbé, Ph.D., is a clinical psychologist and professor of psychology at the University of South Alabama in Mobile, AL, and clinic director of the USA Psychological Clinic. She has published numerous research papers in clinical and health psychology and presents at national and international conferences. Labbé has earned several awards, including the Phi Kappa Phi Scholar of the Year Award, the Ouroboros Award, Who's Who in Biobehavioral Sciences, and university excellence in teaching and service awards. She is the editor in chief of *Journal of Sport Behavior,* is on the editorial board of *Journal of Applied Psychophysiology and Biofeedback,* and has been invited to review a number of clinical and health psychology journals. Labbé teaches and researches mindfulness and has practiced meditation for over thirty years.

Index

professional life mindfulness, 146-147

progress evaluation, 100; for anxiety disorders, 131; for chronic illness, pain, and stress treatment, 126-127; for depression, 135-136; for eating disorders, 142

protocols for treatment. *See* mindfulness-based treatment protocols

psychoeducation: on anxiety, 129; on depression, 132

puppy metaphor, 106-107

R

readings on mindfulness, 157-158

recording mindfulness techniques, 37-38

relapse prevention, 131

relationship enhancement, 113

reliability of tests, 74-75

religion and spirituality, 7-8

research: on effectiveness of MBSR, 121; on formal mindfulness practice, 58; on meditation practice, 18-19; on yoga practice, 70

resources on mindfulness, 157-158

response bias, 76

retreats: couples, 117; mindfulness-based, 39-40, 126

Ricks, D. F., 151

romantic relationships, 31

Ryan, Richard, 9, 16, 84, 87

S

school settings, 155

Schwartz, Gary, 14, 15

Segal, Zindel, 86

self-control, 26

self-regulation, 13-14

self-report mindfulness measures, 82, 84-93; Five Facet Mindfulness Questionnaire,

85-86, 87-88, 90-91; limitations of, 80; Mindful Attention Awareness Scale, 84-85, 87, 89; Toronto Mindfulness Scale, 86, 88, 92-93

sensory exercises, 62-66; on eating, 65-66; on sight, 63-64; on smell, 62-63; on sound, 64; on touch, 64-65

Session Rating Scale (SRS), 97, 151

Shapiro, Shauna, 9, 14, 15

Siegel, Ronald, 5

sight, sense of, 63-64

sitting meditation, 49, 125

smell, sense of, 62-63

Smith, Alastair, 110

Smith, Gregory, 85

social connectedness, 112

social desirability bias, 76

Social Readjustment Rating Scale, 123

social strategies, 29-31; communicating mindfully, 29; enhancing romantic relationships, 31; increasing empathy, 29-31

social validation, 82

somatic relaxation training, 28

sounds, awareness of, 64

Southampton Mindfulness Questionnaire, 86

spirituality, 7-8

sports programs, 154-155

state mindfulness, 3

strategies of mindfulness. *See* mindfulness strategies

stress. *See* chronic illness, pain, and stress

supershrinks, 151-152

Swatmarama, Swami, 67

systematic desensitization, 25

T

taste and satiety meditation, 140

test-retest reliability, 75, 87

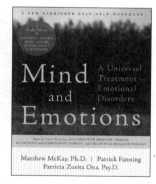